*'I lifted the constitution into the air in the heat of the moment.
I hadn't planned it. I had to do it to show the people that this is it.*

*This is the document that they had struggled for, died for and wept for.*

*This document binds us all together to a common destiny, a common
future and a joint aspiration of what this country could be.'*

**Cyril Ramaphosa**
Chairperson of the Constitutional Assembly

# One**Law**,One**Nation**

The Making of the South African Constitution

Lauren Segal and Sharon Cort

JACANA

First published by Jacana Media (Pty) Ltd in 2011
Second impression 2012

10 Orange Street
Sunnyside
Auckland Park 2092
South Africa
+2711 628 3200
www.jacana.co.za

ISBN 978-1-4314-0270-0

Text © Lauren Segal and Sharon Cort, 2011
Design and layout by Carina Comrie from Bon-Bon and Oliver Barstow
Copy editing by Sandy Shoolman, Russell Martin and Sean Fraser
Cover Image © *Robert Botha*
Set in Interstate and Alexandria
Printed by Ultra Litho (Pty) Ltd
Job no. 001630

The authors have made every endeavour to ensure that copyright
information for the photographs and documents in this book is
accurate and reflects the correct names of the authors of the
documents or the photographers as well as the archival sources.

See a complete list of Jacana titles at www.jacana.co.za

CONSTITUTION HILL TRUST

Even when the environment seems more complex, as it is now – as we work through a period of turbulence – the one thing that we can always say is great about our nation is that we have a universally respected, phenomenal constitution and that document is our shield against anything. Fifteen years later, nothing essential has changed.

The Constitution is as relevant today as it was 15 years ago and it will be as relevant tomorrow. It is the repository of everything, everything that I ever dreamt of, that I ever wanted in my life. It gives me strength, it gives me hope, it protects me. If anyone were ever to violate my rights, our Constitution is my shield.

Never again will courts rubber stamp or stand helplessly by while unjust laws are made to take away peoples' rights, to detain and torture and deny them their dignity. Now judges are champions of the people, testing the actions of the legislatures and the executive against the fine standards we have set ourselves in this Constitution.

This book is a reminder of the long struggle that was fought to give birth to this precious document. It charts the incredible highs and the terrible lows, the immense courage it took to transport this country to that moment 15 years ago when President Nelson Mandela signed the final Constitution into law before the nation and the world.

Cyril Ramaphosa
Chairperson of the Constitutional Assembly

# Foreword by Verne Harris, Nelson Mandela Centre of Memory

There is no doubt that for Nelson Mandela South Africa's 1996 Constitution, together with the rule of law that it underpins, is the jewel in the crown of the country's post-apartheid democratic order.

There is a long reflection by him on the Constitution in the unpublished draft sequel to *Long Walk to Freedom*, which he penned in the period 1998–2002. It comes after a passage detailing political challenges in the era of democracy and the demands on leadership created by these challenges. He continues:

> 'All these considerations, as important as they may be, should never be allowed to undermine our democratic Constitution, which guarantees unqualified citizenship rights to all South Africans ... It has a Bill of Rights on which a citizen can rely if any of his or her rights are threatened or violated. All of us, without exception, are called upon to respect that Constitution.'

Then he moves to the rule of law:

> The apartheid regime had put law and order in disrepute...
>
> ... Because of this crude practice, and out of my own convictions, I exploited every opportunity to promote respect for law and order and for the judiciary.

A passage follows in which he details two instances in which, as President of the country, he was involved in Constitutional Court cases. His conclusion:

> These two examples clearly demonstrated that in the new South Africa there is nobody, not even the President, is above the law, that the rule of law generally, and in particular the independence of the judiciary should be respected.

The reflection ends with an invoking of the imperative to make the Constitution a living reality for all South Africans:

> 'Equally important is the fact that the above considerations should never be an excuse for not addressing the basic demands and needs of our people ...'

The Nelson Mandela Centre of Memory is honoured to have been involved in the production of this book. It at once traces the provenances and antecedents of the Constitution, discloses rich and previously little-used archival resources, documents the many contributors – including Madiba – to the making of the Constitution, and sounds the call for the Constitution to be used as a continuing instrument of liberation. This is a story all South Africans should know and cherish ...

Verne Harris
Nelson Mandela Centre of Memory

# Different Laws for Different Nations

# 1902 - 1989

'The process of negotiating South Africa's first democratic constitution began many years before – long before the African National Congress (ANC) was unbanned in the 1990s, long before the secret meetings between ANC and South African government representatives in the late 1980s. It began when black South Africans first gathered to examine their lot under colonialism, and began to articulate their vision of a different South Africa.'

Cyril Ramaphosa, Chairperson of the Constitutional Assembly

# South Africa's First Three Constitutions

## Overview

South Africa has had five constitutions. The journey towards a negotiated, democratic constitution has a long and complex history that goes back to 1910, when modern South Africa was born. Through the lens of the ever-contested 'non-white franchise' and the genesis of inclusive nationalism, this chapter traces some of the lost opportunities and political dead ends – the moments that could have been and the reconciliations that might have happened – before the 'new South Africa' was born in 1994.

The Treaty of Vereeniging, signed by the British government and the two Boer Republics in 1902, officially ended the bitter and protracted South African War. The two Boer Republics agreed to come under British sovereignty, with the promise of eventual self-government. For the former enemies this was an important if tenuous effort at reconciliation. But for black people, many of whom had fought in the war and were excluded from the peace settlement, this was just the start of the political disempowerment they would endure for the most part of the 20th century.

The Union of South Africa came into being on 31 May 1910 after its first constitution was negotiated at the National Convention of 1908–1909. This signified a new beginning for white South Africans: the British and the Boers were set to become one nation, with black people looking on from the sidelines.

South Africa's first 'colour-bar' constitution was just the beginning of a battery of segregatory laws designed to divide the nation into white citizens and black subjects. With each new legislative act, black people felt increasingly like outcasts in their own country. With each new rebuff, their polite pleas for an inclusive democracy became more outspoken. With each of their demands, the white government became more oppressive.

The most repressive years the country had ever seen followed the adoption of South Africa's Republican Constitution in 1961. After the Soweto uprisings of 1976, people once again took to the streets in protest against the apartheid government and its brutal methods of intimidation. By the early 1980s South Africa had become the pariah of the world and the government realised that apartheid had reached a dead end. The Tricameral Constitution of 1983, which gave a limited political voice to coloureds and Indians, served only to fuel the rage and violence that was engulfing the country at that time.

Eighty-four years after the country's first constitution was adopted, black South Africans were finally able to vote and participate in drawing up the country's first democratic constitution, The Constitution of the Republic of South Africa, 1996.

2

1 Protest march for a new, inclusive constitution.
© UWC / Robben Island Museum / Mayibuye Archives

2 The Treaty of Vereeniging was signed at Melrose House in Pretoria on 31 May 1902. © Ditsong: National Museum of Military History

# South Africa's First Constitution, 1910

[9 EDW. 7.]    *South Africa Act, 1909.*    [CH. **9.**]

## CHAPTER 9.

An Act to constitute the Union of South Africa.    A.D. 1909.
[20th September 1909.]

WHEREAS it is desirable for the welfare and future progress of South Africa that the several British Colonies therein should be united under one Government in a legislative union under the Crown of Great Britain and Ireland :

And whereas it is expedient to make provision for the union of the Colonies of the Cape of Good Hope, Natal, the Transvaal, and the Orange River Colony on terms and conditions to which they have agreed by resolution of their respective Parliaments, and to define the executive, legislative, and judicial powers to be exercised in the government of the Union :

And whereas it is expedient to make provision for the establishment of provinces with powers of legislation and administration in local matters and in such other matters as may be specially reserved for provincial legislation and administration :

And whereas it is expedient to provide for the eventual admission into the Union or transfer to the Union of such parts of South Africa as are not originally included therein :

Be it therefore enacted by the King's most Excellent Majesty, by and with the advice and consent of the Lords Spiritual and Temporal, and Commons, in this present Parliament assembled, and by the authority of the same, as follows :—

### I.—PRELIMINARY.

**1.** This Act may be cited as the South Africa Act, 1909.    Short title.

**2.** In this Act, unless it is otherwise expressed or implied, Definitions.
the words "the Union" shall be taken to mean the Union of

A 4    1

**1** Original version of the preamble to the Union Constitution, adopted on 31 May 1910. © *Parliament of South Africa*

**2** Original signed version of the 1910 Constitution. © *Parliament of South Africa*

# A divided nationhood

1908 - 1910

*'We who love South Africa as a whole, who have our ideal of her, who wish to substitute the idea of a United South Africa for the lost independence, who see in breadth of horizon and in a wider, more embracing statesmanship the cure for many of our ills and the only escape from the dreary pettiness and bickerings of the past, we are prepared to sacrifice so much: not to Natal or the Cape, but to South Africa.'* - General Jan Smuts

Far from creating the unified nation imagined in Smuts's rhetoric, South Africa's first constitution entrenched racial discrimination and the deep divisions in South African society. When delegates from all four provinces met to draft a new constitution at the National Convention of 1908-9, they were also giving shape to the idea of nationhood. For most of the delegates the nation imagined was an exclusively white nation. Black people, who were excluded from the process, watched as their future was decided for them.

Many compromises were made to ensure that the ingrained mistrust between the Boers and the British didn't undermine the negotiation process. On the issue of union or federation, Smuts argued, successfully, that the former would facilitate greater unity between the former enemies and encourage loyalty through shared symbols and national identity:

*'The Native Delegates from different parts of Natal, while highly appreciating the Government's desire and intention to give the Native people of the Colony of Natal Parliamentary representation by the nomination of four members to represent them in the Legislative Council, would most respectfully point out that such members cannot be truly said to be their representatives but Nominees of the Governor in Council; and would, therefore most humbly beg to ask for the extension of the Franchise to the Native Races of this Colony.'*

1

2

3

a PUBLIC MEETING held under the Auspices of the COLOURED
PEOPLES' ASSOCIATION on the 8th of March, 1909, the
following "RESOLUTION" was carried unanimously :-

THE ANALYSIS of the SOUTH AFRICAN DRAFT
CONSTITUTION.

This meeting of coloured people of Beaufort West,
Cape Colony, having considered the Draft Constitution
as printed, finds that the Constitution recommends
the plucking up by the roots of three horns of this
Monster Empire (rendered so through the doings of
33 men) viz :- 1st. that styled "of European descent";
2nd. the coloured people of the Cape Colony; 3rd. the
Kaffir races; and to raise up in their stead a new
horn whose advent is to be proclaimed by the taking
of a Census of the European population only (Vide
Article 33 (11)), and the votes and citizen rights
of the residue to cease either through death or a
two-third majority of the Union Parliament (Vide
Article 35). Then it also recommends the doing away
of the British Diadem (Vide Article 44 (c)) and
(Article 25 (d & e)). This meeting respectfully
wish to call the attention of the Imperial Parliament to the fact that the Royal Diadem of Japan con-
sists of 50 million units, of which the Mikado is the
centre unit, the whole being governed by one measure
viz :- a measure of wheat for one penny and three
measures of barley for a penny, not for any one class,
but for the whole 50 million, including the Emperor;
therefore the meeting urges the Imperial Parliament
to revert strictly to British Customs and Principles,
as far as the South African Draft Constitution is
concerned, so that here, as in Japan, the whole population may form a living part of a real Diadem, and
not of a Crown made of gold, mixed with a baser
metal, which the 33 men seem to think is the British
Diadem.

Lastly, this meeting is confident that the Coloured
people can form a few articles themselves which could
be embodied in the Draft Constitution. Failing this,
the meeting must ask that the Preamble to the Draft
Constitution reads thus :-

One Government, to administer one law for
one people, namely, a British People.

(SGD). J. ANTONY,
(Chairman).

The pleading petitions submitted by black people to air their grievances and set out their demands in a gentlemanly fashion were all but ignored. Although some Cape and Natal liberals argued for their colonies' qualified, colour-blind franchise (then referred to as the non-white franchise) to be extended to the former Boer Republics, the majority of delegates were opposed to this. In the end the Convention decided that each province would retain its existing franchise system and that membership of Parliament would be restricted to 'British subjects of European descent', even in the Cape. FS Malan, one of the more committed Cape liberals, spoke prophetically of the years of conflict that would ensue from this decision.

*'People spoke about the necessity to unite the white races first and then tackle the Native franchise question but a union of this kind would not be a genuine union. The germs of discord would continue to exist.'*

The proposed Union Parliament was based on the Westminster system, making the legislature, consisting in South Africa's case of the House of Assembly and the Senate, supreme in authority. This meant that Parliament, elected by the white minority, could enact any laws it chose subject to the assent of the Governor-General. The founding constitution, the South Africa Act, could also be amended by a majority vote in both Houses of Parliament, but changing the voting requirements enshrined in the Act required a two-thirds majority. The judiciary could only interpret legislation, not comment on its legality or determine whether laws passed were just or not. In the years to come, the apartheid regime used this form of government to its advantage, enacting Draconian laws that stripped away people's rights in every part of their lives.

1 General Jan Smuts, the main architect of the first Constitution.
1925. © *Museum Africa*

2 Dinner menu from the National Convention, which held its first
meeting in Durban in October 1908. © *Museum Africa*

3 Delegates at the National Convention 1908-9. © *Museum Africa*

4 Petition from the Coloured People's Association in protest against
the draft constitution, 8 March 1909. © *National Library, Cape Town*

The South Africa Act outraged both black and liberal-minded white people. AK Soga, editor of *Izwi Labantu* (Voice of the People), wrote: *'This is treachery! It is worse. It is successful betrayal, for the Act has virtually disenfranchised the black man already even before the meeting of the Union Parliament, which will complete the crime by the solemn vote of the two Assemblies.'*

William Schreiner, a former Cape Prime Minister and member of a liberal family, led a deputation to England in 1909 to try to persuade the British government not to pass the draft South Africa Act. Their attempts were unsuccessful. On 20 September 1909, the British Parliament passed the South Africa Act, which effectively became South Africa's first constitution when the Union came about on 31 May 1910. This was the beginning of a constitutional and political system that would effectively create two different nations governed by two different sets of laws.

1

# Union Day

## 31 May
## 1910

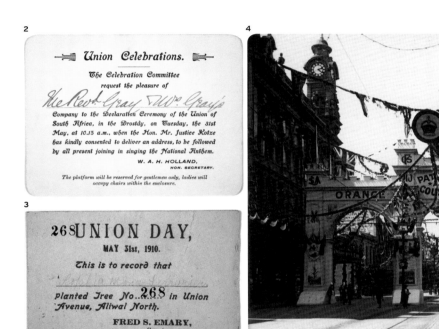

**1** The Schreiner Delegation. 1909. © *National Library, Cape Town*

**2-3** Invitation and tree-planting stub, Union Day, 31 May 1910. © *Museum Africa*

**4** The Orange Free State decorates its streets in celebration of Union Day, 31 May 1910. © *Museum Africa*

**5** A procession escorting the first Governor-General of the Union to the Opening of the first Union Parliament. November 1910. © *National Library, Cape Town*

# Opening of Parliament

4 November
1910

**1** A guard of honour marks the Opening of Parliament,
Cape Town. 1910. © *Parliament of South Africa*

**2** The first cabinet of the Union of South Africa. 1910.
© *National Archives and Records Service of South Africa*

**3** HRH the Duke of Connaught and his wife leave
Parliament. 1910. © *Parliament of South Africa*

**4** HRH the Duke of Connaught opens the first Union
Parliament. 4 November 1910. © *Parliament of South Africa*

1

# Separate nationalisms

1910 - 1940

In spite of Union in 1910, South Africa's parliamentary and constitutional history was very much a story of the struggle for supremacy between the Boers and Brits, the white English and Afrikaans speakers of the land, but they were for the most part a united white front in their repression of the black majority. Ultimately Afrikaner nationalism, represented by the National Party, which was formed in 1914, triumphed.

Outside formal political processes, African nationalism also gathered force. In 1911 one of the leaders of the new movement, Pixley Seme, called for a congress that would represent the national interests of black people in South Africa and wrote in *Imvo Zabantsundu* (Black Opinion): *'The demon of racialism, the aberrations of the Xosa-Fingo feud, the animosity that exists between Zulus and the Tongans, between the Basutos and every other Native, must be buried and forgotten; it has shed among us sufficient blood! We are one people. These divisions, these jealousies, are the cause of all our woes and of all our backwardness and ignorance today.'*

One year later, in 1912, several hundred delegates came together to form the South African Native National Congress (SANNC), later renamed the African National Congress (ANC), the first national political organisation for black people in South Africa. The founders of the SANNC were moderate, mission-schooled intellectuals who mistakenly believed that they could effect constitutional change by appealing to the innate sense of justice and fairness of the British. Their repeated attempts to be heard failed and in the 1920s and 1930s the ANC became largely ineffectual as an organisation. Many working-class black people perceived the ANC to be elitist and joined the more radical Industrial and Commercial Workers' Union (ICU) of South Africa and also the Communist Party of South Africa (CPSA). In the 1920s the CPSA youth league began actively campaigning for black members in response to the slogan of the 1922 white miners' strike: 'Workers of the world, unite and fight for a white South Africa!.'

In the mid-1930s the black political classes were galvanised into action when the Prime Minister, General Hertzog, presented his 'Native Bills' to Parliament. The bills sought, among other things, to abolish the African franchise in the Cape and thereby take away the last vestige of black political rights. In the largest show of support the country had seen, five hundred delegates from different black political organisations met at the All African Convention (AAC) in 1935 to deliberate on Hertzog's Bills. In the end, however, despite protests and petitions, the Bills were passed in 1936 and Africans lost direct representation in Parliament. As devastating as the Bills were, Selby Msimang, Secretary-General of the AAC proclaimed: *'I see in this crisis the hand of Fate stretching out to free us. General Hertzog and all his lieutenants may prove yet the instruments by which we will forge our liberation. Bantudom now sees the clouds gathering on the horizon and seeks to gather her children under her strong wings. Shall we prove cowards and flee from her strength? God forbids.'*

1

16

## ORANGE FREE STATE.

*Specific Cases of Evictions under the Natives.*

*Land Act 1913 District Kroonstad.*

*Natives.*　　*Farms*

Stephen Moraba, Rienzi :—Evicted have tive stock in large quantity.

Jacob Maphike do.—Evicted gone to Basutoland with stock and ,amily.

Fillard Chaka, do.—Evicted Has sent stock to Basutaland.

Zachariah Doge, Theron :—Evicted now wandering with 20 cattle and 40 sheep and family.

Johannes Pali Vlakkuil :—Evicted now wandering with 100 sheep, 14 cattle and family.

Sethologo Zloego Morabe Driekapys :— Evicted now wandering with stock and family.

Anbooi Molele, Patregsdraai :—Evicted but returned under labour conditions after selling all stock at aloss.

Jantje Ventersberg, Winburg :—Evicted given notice to leave farm in 8 days.

Indicate signed statement verifying circumstances of Eviction.

Jankil Kgaile, Onderwag :—Evicted wandering with stock.

# The Freedom Charter

## We, the People of South Africa, declare for all our country and the world to know:

that South Africa belongs to all who live in it, black and white, and that no government can justly claim authority unless it is based on the will of all the people;

that our people have been robbed of their birthright to land, liberty and peace by a form of government founded on injustice and inequality;

that our country will never be prosperous or free until all our people live in brotherhood, enjoying equal rights and opportunities;

that only a democratic state, based on the will of all the people, can secure to all their birthright without distinction of colour, race, sex or belief;

And therefore, we, the people of South Africa, black and white together—equals, countrymen and brothers—adopt this Freedom Charter. And we pledge ourselves to strive together, sparing neither strength nor courage, until the democratic changes here set out have been won.

### THE PEOPLE SHALL GOVERN!

Every man and woman shall have the right to vote for and to stand as a candidate for all bodies which make laws;

All people shall be entitled to take part in the administration of the country;

The rights of the people shall be the same, regardless of race, colour or sex;

All bodies of minority rule, advisory boards, councils and authorities shall be replaced by democratic organs of self-government.

### ALL NATIONAL GROUPS SHALL HAVE EQUAL RIGHTS!

There shall be equal status in the bodies of state, in the courts and in the schools for all national groups and races;

All people shall have equal right to use their own languages, and to develop their own folk culture and customs;

All national groups shall be protected by law against insults to their race and national pride;

The preaching and practice of national, race or colour discrimination and contempt shall be a punishable crime;

All apartheid laws and practices shall be set aside.

### THE PEOPLE SHALL SHARE IN THE COUNTRY'S WEALTH!

The national wealth of our country, the heritage of all South Africans, shall be restored to the people;

The mineral wealth beneath the soil, the Banks and monopoly industry shall be transferred to the ownership of the people as a whole;

All other industry and trade shall be controlled to assist the well-being of the people;

All people shall have equal rights to trade where they choose, to manufacture and to enter all trades, crafts and professions.

### THE LAND SHALL BE SHARED AMONG THOSE WHO WORK IT!

Restrictions of land ownership on a racial basis shall be ended, and all the land redivided amongst those who work it, to banish famine and land hunger;

The state shall help the peasants with implements, seed, tractors and dams to save the soil and assist the tillers;

Freedom of movement shall be guaranteed to all who work on the land;

All shall have the right to occupy land wherever they choose;

People shall not be robbed of their cattle, and forced labour and farm prisons shall be abolished.

### ALL SHALL BE EQUAL BEFORE THE LAW!

No one shall be imprisoned, deported or restricted without a fair trial;

No one shall be condemned by the order of any Government official;

The courts shall be representative of all the people;

Imprisonment shall be only for serious crimes against the people, and shall aim at re-education, not vengeance;

The police force and army shall be open to all on an equal basis and shall be the helpers and protectors of the people;

All laws which discriminate on grounds of race, colour or belief shall be repealed.

### ALL SHALL ENJOY EQUAL HUMAN RIGHTS!

The law shall guarantee to all their right to speak, to organise, to meet together, to publish, to preach, to worship and to educate their children;

The privacy of the house from police raids shall be protected by law;

All shall be free to travel without restriction from countryside to town, from province to province, and from South Africa abroad;

Pass Laws, permits and all other laws restricting these freedoms shall be abolished.

### THERE SHALL BE WORK AND SECURITY!

All who work shall be free to form trade unions, to elect their officers and to make wage agreements with their employers;

The state shall recognise the right and duty of all to work, and to draw full unemployment benefits;

Men and women of all races shall receive equal pay for equal work;

There shall be a forty-hour working week, a national minimum wage, paid annual leave, and sick leave for all workers, and maternity leave on full pay for all working mothers;

Miners, domestic workers, farm workers and civil servants shall have the same rights as all others who work;

Child labour, compound labour, the tot system and contract labour shall be abolished.

### THE DOORS OF LEARNING AND OF CULTURE SHALL BE OPENED!

The government shall discover, develop and encourage national talent for the enhancement of our cultural life;

All the cultural treasures of mankind shall be open to all, by free exchange of books, ideas and contact with other lands;

The aim of education shall be to teach the youth to love their people and their culture, to honour human brotherhood, liberty and peace;

Education shall be free, compulsory, universal and equal for all children;

Higher education and technical training shall be opened to all by means of state allowances and scholarships awarded on the basis of merit;

Adult illiteracy shall be ended by a mass state education plan;

Teachers shall have all the rights of other citizens;

The colour bar in cultural life, in sport and in education shall be abolished.

### THERE SHALL BE HOUSES, SECURITY AND COMFORT!

All people shall have the right to live where they choose, to be decently housed, and to bring up their families in comfort and security;

Unused housing space to be made available to the people;

Rent and prices shall be lowered, food plentiful and no one shall go hungry;

A preventive health scheme shall be run by the state;

Free medical care and hospitalisation shall be provided for all, with special care for mothers and young children;

Slums shall be demolished, and new suburbs built where all have transport, roads, lighting, playing fields, creches and social centres;

The aged, the orphans, the disabled and the sick shall be cared for by the state;

Rest, leisure and recreation shall be the right of all;

Fenced locations and ghettoes shall be abolished, and laws which break up families shall be repealed.

### THERE SHALL BE PEACE AND FRIENDSHIP!

South Africa shall be a fully independent state, which respects the rights and sovereignty of all nations;

South Africa shall strive to maintain world peace and the settlement of all international disputes by negotiation—not war;

Peace and friendship amongst all our people shall be secured by upholding the equal rights, opportunities and status of all;

The people of the protectorates—Basutoland, Bechuanaland and Swaziland shall be free to decide for themselves their own future;

The right of all the peoples of Africa to independence and self-government shall be recognised, and shall be the basis of close co-operation.

*Let all who love their people and their country now say, as we say here: "THESE FREEDOMS WE WILL FIGHT FOR, SIDE BY SIDE, THROUGHOUT OUR LIVES, UNTIL WE HAVE WON OUR LIBERTY."*

Adopted at the Congress of the People, Kliptown, South Africa, on 26th June, 1955.

Royal 1259

# Many nations, one land

## 1955-1960

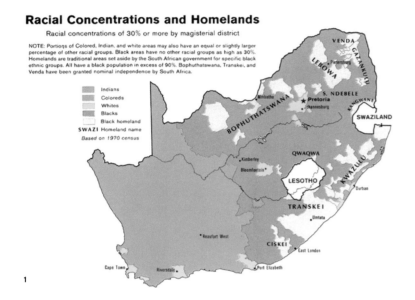

**Racial Concentrations and Homelands**

Racial concentrations of 30% or more by magisterial district

NOTE: Portions of Colored, Indian, and white areas may also have an equal or slightly larger percentage of other racial groups. Black areas have no other racial groups as high as 30%. Homelands are traditional areas set aside by the South African government for specific black ethnic groups. All have a black population in excess of 90%. Bophuthatswana, Transkei, and Venda have been granted nominal independence by South Africa.

- Indians
- Coloreds
- Whites
- Blacks
- Black homeland
- **SWAZI** Homeland name

Based on 1970 census

1

Three years later when Dr HF Verwoerd became Prime Minister he made it quite clear that the Freedom Charter meant nothing to him. In effect he used the Bantu Self-Government Act of 1959 to deal with the issue of political rights for black South Africans. The Act forced them to become 'citizens of another country', that is citizens of specially designated, 'autonomous' homelands with their own governments and impoverished economies. Verwoerd called this a policy of 'good neighbourliness' and a 'supremely positive step' towards placing Africans 'on the road to self-government'. But in a speech to the Senate in 1959 he said: *'I choose an assured White state in South Africa, whatever happens to the other areas, rather than to have my people absorbed in one integrated state in which the Bantu must eventually dominate.'* In reality the homelands policy was just another means of excluding black people from the political and constitutional life of South Africa.

2

**1** Racial-demographic map of South Africa published by the CIA in 1979, with data from the South African census.

**2** Leader of the PAC, Robert Sobukwe, leads supporters to the police station at the start of their campaign against the pass laws, 21 March 1960.
© *Bailey's African History Archives / Africa Media Online*

**3** Police open fire on protestors at Sharpeville killing 69 people, 21 March 1960. © *Museum Africa*

**4** More than 5000 people attend the funeral of the victims of the Sharpeville Massacre, May 1960. © *Bailey's African History Archives / Africa Media Online*

On 21 March 1960, the police opened fire on a group of peaceful anti-pass protestors at Sharpeville, killing 69 and injuring more than 100. The government responded by banning both the ANC and the Pan Africanist Congress (PAC). Seeing no other way of countering state violence, the ANC, together with the SACP and other organisations, announced the formation of a military wing, Umkhonto we Sizwe/MK on 16 December 1961. In the years that followed many leaders were jailed or else they fled into exile to rally international support or receive military training for the armed struggle.

It would take another 40 years of oppression, struggle and bloodshed for the ringing declaration of the Freedom Charter to be realised and embodied in a democratic constitution.

# South Africa's Second Constitution, 1961

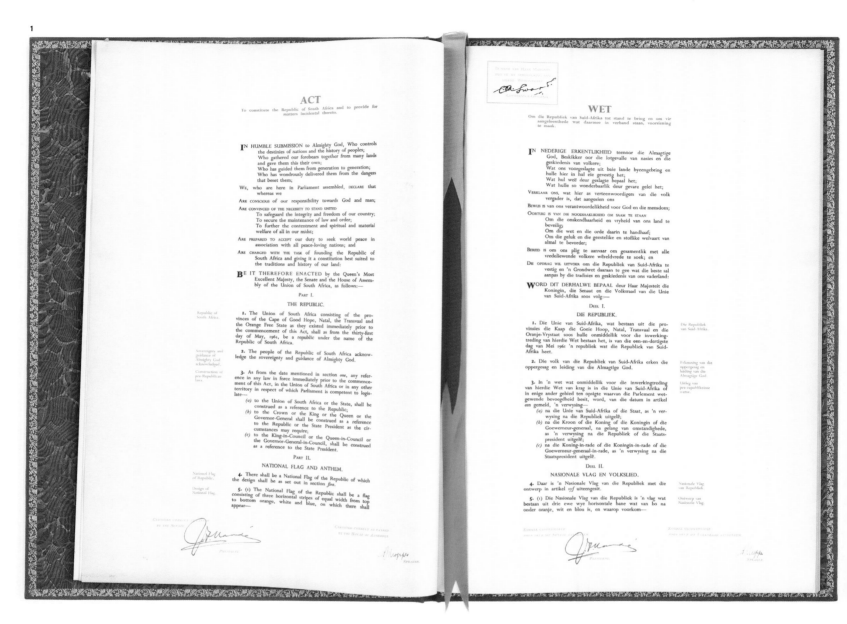

1

**1** Original Preamble to the Republican Constitution,
adopted on 31 May 1961. © *Parliament of South Africa*

**2** Original Government Gazette of the Republic of
South Africa Act. © *Parliament of South Africa*

**Republiek van Suid-Afrika** ◆ **Republic of South Africa**

# Buitengewone
# Staatskoerant
# Government Gazette
## Extraordinary

*(As 'n Nuusblad by die Poskantoor Geregistreer)*     *(Registered at the Post Office as a Newspaper)*

| Vol. I.] | PRYS 5c. | PRETORIA, 31 MEI 31 MAY 1961. | PRICE 5c. | [No. 1. |

## *Proklamasie*

### VAN DIE STAATSPRESIDENT VAN DIE REPUBLIEK VAN SUID-AFRIKA.

No. 1, 1961.]

### AANVAARDING VAN DIE AMP VAN STAATSPRESIDENT.

Nademaal ek op 10 Mei 1961 ingevolge die bepalings van die Grondwet van die Republiek van Suid-Afrika, 1961, behoorlik verkose verklaar is as Staatspresident van die Republiek van Suid-Afrika en vandag die voorgeskrewe Ampseed in daardie hoedanigheid afgelê het;

So is dit dat ek hierby verklaar dat ek vandag die genoemde Amp van Staatspresident van die Republiek van Suid-Afrika, met al die bevoegdhede, pligte en funksies daaraan verbonde, aanvaar het, waarvan hierby kennis gegee word aan alle Ministers en beamptes van die genoemde Republiek, aan Suid-Afrikaanse burgers en alle ander persone wat dit mag aangaan en van wie dit vereis word dat hulle daarvan behoorlik kennis moet neem.

Gegee onder my Hand en die Seël van die Republiek van Suid-Afrika te Pretoria, op hierdie Een-en-dertigste dag van Mei Eenduisend Negehonderd Een-en-sestig.

**C. R. SWART,**
Staatspresident.

Op las van die Staatspresident-in-rade.

**H. F. VERWOERD.**

## *Proclamation*

### BY THE STATE PRESIDENT OF THE REPUBLIC OF SOUTH AFRICA.

No. 1, 1961.]

### ASSUMPTION OF OFFICE OF STATE PRESIDENT.

Whereas, on the 10th May, 1961, I was declared to be duly elected as State President of the Republic of South Africa under the provisions of the Republic of South Africa Constitution Act, 1961, and have this day made and subscribed the prescribed Oath of Office in that capacity;

Now, therefore, I do hereby declare that I have this day assumed the said Office of State President of the Republic of South Africa, with all the powers, duties and functions pertaining thereto, of which notice is hereby given to all Ministers and officers of the said Republic, to South African citizens and all other persons whom it may concern and who are required to take due notice thereof.

Given under my Hand and the Seal of the Republic of South Africa at Pretoria on this Thirty-first day of May, One thousand Nine hundred and Sixty-one.

**C. R. SWART,**
State President.

By Order of the State President-in-Council.

**H. F. VERWOERD.**

| S. A. MYBURGH, Staatsdrukker, Pretoria. | S. A. MYBURGH, Government Printer, Pretoria. |

A—1411172

# *Republiek of Unie?* Republic or Union?

1960

Verwoerd's dream was to turn South Africa into a Republic ruled by the Afrikaner and free from British interference. This would allow the South African government to deal with its 'native problem' in whatever way it chose, without reference to the British Crown. An all-white referendum held on 5 October 1960 indicated that 52 per cent of white citizens were in favour of a Republic. With this mandate, Verwoerd passed legislation to turn the Union into the Republic of South Africa. Having made this constitutional change, Verwoerd was obliged to request from fellow members of the British Commonwealth that South Africa remain a member. His request, however, met with so much antagonism because of South Africa's policy of apartheid that Verwoerd withdrew his application saying: *'No self-respecting member of any voluntary organisation could, in view of … the degree of interference shown in what are South Africa's domestic affairs, be expected to wish to retain membership in what is now becoming a pressure group.'*

One month before South Africa was declared a Republic, Nelson Mandela made a last effort to stop the process. Although the ANC was banned at the time, the organisation continued to campaign for constitutional rights from its underground headquarters. In a letter to Verwoerd, Mandela reminded him of the demands of the ANC and its allies for a national convention of elected representatives *'on an equal basis irrespective of race, colour, creed or other limitation'* to decide on a new non-racial democratic constitution for South Africa. As he said, *'No Constitution or form of Government decided without the participation of the African people who form an absolute majority of the population can enjoy moral validity or merit support either within South Africa or beyond its borders.'*

Verwoerd did not respond. The All-in African Conference called for a three-day stay-at-home and received massive support throughout the country, but still the government didn't budge.

Nelson Mandela had anticipated that they wouldn't be successful, but wanted to draw international attention to their demands. In a statement after the stay-at-home he said: *'Ever since the All-in African Conference at Pietermaritzburg, the issue that dominated South African politics and that attracted pressmen from all over the world was not the Republican celebrations organised by the government, but the stirring campaign of the African people and other non-White sections to mark our rejection of a White Republic forcibly imposed upon us by a minority. Few political organisations could have succeeded in conducting such a stubborn and relentless campaign under conditions which, for all practical purposes, amounted to martial law. But we did.'*

On 31 May 1961, the last day of the stayaway, South Africa became a Republic.

1

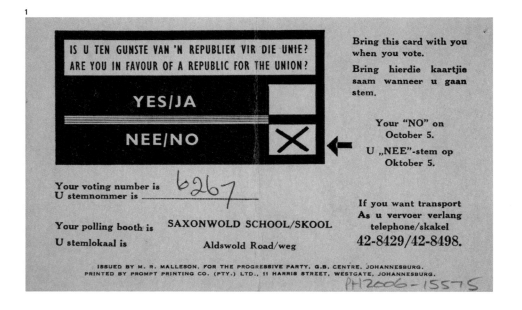

1 Voter registration card for the 1960 referendum.
© *Museum Africa*

2 HF Verwoed outside Parliament, 22 March 1961.
© *National Library, Cape Town*

3 Mandela addresses the All-in African Conference
in Pietermaritzburg, May 1961. © *Bailey's African
History Archives / Africa Media Online*

# Becoming a Republic

31 May
1961

The Republic of South Africa Constitution Act, 1961 came into force on 31 May 1961. This, South Africa's second constitution, was largely unchanged from its first. In becoming a Republic, South Africa cut all ties with the British Crown. The word 'State' was substituted whenever 'King', 'Queen' or 'Crown' appeared in legal documents. Queen's Counsels became known as Senior Counsels; the 'Royal' title was dropped from the names of some South African regiments; and rands and cents replaced pounds, shillings and pence. But the parliamentary system remained unchanged and the Union flag remained the national flag of South Africa until 1994.

As a conciliatory gesture to English-speaking whites opposed to a Republic, there was no executive presidency. The authority of the British Crown and Governor-General was merged into a new position, that of State President, who was elected by Parliament but had very little real power and performed mainly ceremonial duties.

Coloured voters were finally removed from the common voters' roll and were placed on a separate list in 1956. They became entitled to vote for a small number of white MPs to represent their interests. In 1968, even these indirect representatives were abolished, leaving both the Senate and the House of Assembly to represent white voters only. Instead, a Coloured Persons' Representative Council (CPRC) consisting of 40 elected coloured representatives and 20 nominated white members was instituted. The council would be able to pass laws about parochial matters affecting coloured people. The CPRC proved largely ineffectual, and was but a prelude to the equally ineffectual Tricameral Parliament, created in 1983.

# The years of repression

1961 - 1980

A sense of foreboding had marked the start of the 1960s. The decade was to be the most repressive the country had ever experienced. After a period of relative quiescence, the 1976 Soweto student uprising on 16 June, in which over 500 people died and thousands were arrested, heralded an era of increasingly militant mass struggle and youth activism. ANC President, Oliver Tambo, was resolute when he addressed the UN three months later: *'The blood that our people have shed calls for action, not for more words. It calls for action to destroy the fascist regime that continues to massacre the innocent.'*

By the time PW Botha was appointed Prime Minister in late 1978, South Africa had become the pariah of the world. The international community had begun to boycott South African products and sporting events. MK soldiers were increasingly infiltrating the country and launching small-scale attacks. Botha responded with a series of cross-border raids into the already hostile neighbouring states. At the same time, realising that apartheid was hurtling towards a dead end, he announced that he was planning a series of reforms. In typically autocratic mode Botha bluntly told conservative whites to 'adapt or die' and later made it clear to 'radicals' who 'play around with music from Lusaka' that he would not countenance opposition or give in to their demands for 'one man, one vote'.

**1** After being sworn in, State President CR Swart is accompanied by a mounted escort to Church Square in Pretoria, 31 May 1961.

**2** Schoolchildren protesting against Bantu Education leading to the start of the Soweto Uprisings on 16 June 1976. © Peter Magubane

**3** A demonstration in Australia against the South African team. © Bailey's African History Archives / Africa Media Online

# South Africa's Third Constitution, 1983

1

| 2 | No. 8914 | GOVERNMENT GAZETTE, 28 SEPTEMBER 1983 |
|---|---|---|

**Act No. 110, 1983**     REPUBLIC OF SOUTH AFRICA CONSTITUTION ACT, 1983

## ACT

**To introduce a new constitution for the Republic of South Africa and to provide for matters incidental thereto.**

---

*(English text signed by the State President.)*
*(Assented to 22 September 1983.)*

---

IN HUMBLE SUBMISSION to Almighty God, Who controls the destinies of peoples and nations,
Who gathered our forebears together from many lands and gave them this their own,
Who has guided them from generation to generation,
Who has wondrously delivered them from the dangers that beset them,

WE DECLARE that we
ARE CONSCIOUS of our responsibility towards God and man;
ARE CONVINCED of the necessity of standing united and of pursuing the following national goals:

To uphold Christian values and civilized norms, with recognition and protection of freedom of faith and worship,
To safeguard the integrity and freedom of our country,
To uphold the independence of the judiciary and the equality of all under the law,
To secure the maintenance of law and order,
To further the contentment and the spiritual and material welfare of all,
To respect and to protect the human dignity, life, liberty and property of all in our midst,
To respect, to further and to protect the self-determination of population groups and peoples,
To further private initiative and effective competition;

ARE PREPARED TO ACCEPT our duty to seek world peace in association with all peace-loving peoples and nations; and

ARE DESIROUS OF GIVING THE REPUBLIC OF SOUTH AFRICA A CONSTITUTION which provides for elected and responsible forms of government and which is best suited to the traditions, history and circumstances of our land:

BE IT THEREFORE ENACTED by the State President and the House of Assembly of the Republic of South Africa, as follows:—

**1** Preamble to the Tricameral Constitution, adopted on 22 September 1983.
© *Parliament of South Africa*

**2** President PW Botha takes a salute during a military parade. © *Paul Weinberg / Africa Media Online*

# Dismounting the tiger

By the early 1980s, the struggle had intensified in the country. Grassroots protest was gaining momentum, the unions were demonstrating their might through mass action and state agents were attempting to stifle the growing protest with intimidation and violence. Angry black South Africans demanded that white South Africans get off 'the tiger of white domination'. FW de Klerk, former President of South Africa, has said, *'PW Botha's response to the question of how one dismounts a tiger was that one does it quite gingerly – one foot at a time – with as much military fire-power as one can muster.'*

It was in this heated political climate that Botha put his first foot forward and revealed his plan for a Tricameral Parliament in 1983. This would introduce coloured and Indian people into the all-white Parliament, giving them direct but limited representation. There was a fierce reaction. White conservatives who feared the demise of apartheid hastily set about forming the Conservative Party and people excluded from the new arrangement or opposed to its racially charged nature protested that apartheid had to be scrapped not reformed.

For the majority of South Africans Botha's reforms were too little and too late. The country was on fire and the 'one foot at a time' approach of Botha served to stoke the fire.

Of major significance for the future was the launch of the United Democratic Front (UDF), a mass-based popular front of oppositional bodies and organisations that took the country by storm.

2

# 'We want it all and we want it now!'

At the launch of the UDF in Cape Town on 20 August 1983, the Rev. Allan Boesak gave a rousing speech in which he told Botha that the majority of the country's people had lost patience with his reforms.

*'We want all our rights and we want them here and we want them now. We have been waiting for too long. We have been struggling for too long and now I hear people admonishing us saying, "You are in too much of a hurry, can't you see that the government is making progress. There are changes on the way" and they are saying that we must be a little patient and that we must cool off, but I fear that if we keep on cooling off we may end up in the deep freeze. The world knows that we have been patient, we have waited for many years, we have pleaded, we have tried, we have petitioned for so long, we have been jailed and exiled and killed for so long, but we are saying today, "Now is the time."'*

Botha paid no heed to the demands of the UDF, but concerned that he may lose the support of the white electorate, held an all-white referendum on 2 November 1983. Some 70 per cent of white voters voted in favour of the Tricameral Parliament.

The deed was done but opposition continued. In January 1984, the UDF organised the Million Signatures Campaign, the first nationwide campaign in opposition to apartheid for decades. Boycotts, strikes, marches and pamphleteering followed. Five days before the general elections for the Tricameral Parliament were held in August 1984, the United Nations adopted Resolution 554, condemning the new system and declaring the elections for it 'null and void'.

All the same, the elections went ahead. A number of coloured and Indian parties participated, but the low voter turnout especially among these communities suggested that the majority of people were opposed. The new Parliament met for the first time on 3 September 1984, but the UDF had nonetheless sent a strong message to the government about the strength of 'people's power' and the efficacy of mass action.

# A fundamantal lack of democracy

1983

'The [1983] Constitution lacked substantive principle, constitutionalism and even a regard for the rule of law. It failed to protect individual rights, showed a fundamental lack of democracy, lacked an independent judiciary, did not have adequate checks and balances, had no minority protections and gave excessive power to the President.'
– South African Law Commission

The convoluted Tricameral Parliament comprised three chambers of Parliament: a (white) House of Assembly, a (coloured) House of Representatives, and an (Indian) House of Delegates. In terms of the new constitution, each of the three racially separate chambers of the Tricameral Parliament would determine laws relating to its group's 'own affairs' such as education, health, housing, social welfare and local government. 'General affairs' such as defence, justice, finance and foreign policy needed the approval of all three chambers. Any differences or disputes between the chambers would be resolved by a President's Council, so giving the white House (the largest of the three) or rather the National Party the upper hand in decision-making. Power was left firmly in white hands. Seventy-four years after Union black South Africans were still excluded from representation in this system and had to exercise their political rights in the homelands where they were forced to be 'citizens'.

As part of the constitutional changes effected in 1983, the position of Prime Minister was abolished and PW Botha became the first executive State President of South Africa. Being both the head of the National Party and of the government gave him enormous power, which was wielded ferociously against popular opposition to the regime in the 1980s.

**1** The UDF is launched on 20 August 1983. © *Rashid Lombard*

**2** Albertina Sisulu leads a meeting of the UDF in Johannesburg in the mid-1980s. © *Paul Weinberg*

**3** Members of the (coloured) House of Representatives arrive to take their place in the Assembly Chamber, 17 September 1984. © *National Archives of South Africa*

**4** State President PW Botha delivers his opening speech in the Volksraad during the official Opening of Parliament, Cape Town, 31 January 1986. © *National Archives and Record Service of South Africa*

# On the edge of an abyss

1985

By the mid-1980s the country was burning. Two events in 1985 pushed South Africa to the edge of the abyss. On 20 July 1985 Botha introduced the first of two states of emergency, which gave the police and the army excessive power to 'restore law and order'. The ANC President, Oliver Tambo, hit back on Radio Freedom by calling for South Africa's 25 million black people *'to make apartheid unworkable and our country ungovernable'*. The international community put further pressure on the government to end apartheid.

On 15 August 1985 Botha made his infamous 'Rubicon speech'. Pik Botha, then Minister of Foreign Affairs, had led the world to believe that the President would be announcing sweeping changes, including the release of Nelson Mandela who had earlier in the year refused Botha's offer of a conditional release. But Botha, unlike Caesar, failed to cross the Rubicon. Instead he said to the world, 'Don't push us too far.'

Once again Oliver Tambo entered the battle from exile to comment on Botha's arrogant speech. *'At a time when every thinking person in our country and abroad is saying apartheid must end now, the ruling group could not help but show itself for what it is – a clique of diehard racists, hidebound reactionaries and bloodthirsty fascist braggarts who will heed nobody except themselves.'*

**1** Society's most vulnerable feel the effects of the increasing violence. 1 January 1985. © *UN Photo / Peter Magubane*

**2** Oliver Tambo, ANC President, and Thabo Mbeki, Publicity Secretary, and Alfred Nzo, Secretary-General, during the ANC's 74th Anniversary press conference in Lusaka, Zambia. 9 January 1986. © *Gallo Images / Ken Owen*

**3** Mourners at a funeral for those who were killed by the South African Police at Langa Township in Uitenhage. 1 March 1985. © *UN Photo*

As early as 1983 the National Intelligence Service (NIS) had approached President Botha to advise him that a negotiated settlement was the only answer to the conflict-ridden situation in South Africa. Niël Barnard, head of the NIS at the time, recalls:

*'It was quite clear that the only way to tackle that was to start talking in some way or another with Mr Mandela in person. I started discussions with President Botha, the Prime Minister at the time, saying that we have to find a negotiated settlement. We have to find a way out of increasing civil conflict.'*

Botha was losing his footing, but he was determined not to appear weak in the face of international disinvestment, a falling rand, local boycotts, spiralling violence and attacks on strategic targets by the armed militants in the resistance. The turmoil in the country and Botha's stubborn belligerence belied the fact that secret talks were already underway between Nelson Mandela and the government.

In 1984 Botha authorised the Justice Minister, Kobie Coetsee, to meet with Mandela to discuss various issues. Coetsee was impressed with Mandela's charismatic presence when he met him in 1985: *'He was clearly in command of his immediate surroundings. We almost buried the past immediately. It was the beginning of the exercise to defuse, to talk, rather than to fight.'* Secret meetings to establish if there was enough common ground to initiate peace talks continued throughout the rest of the 1980s.

# Another clampdown

1986 - 1987

Back in Parliament, Botha began cautiously abolishing some petty apartheid legislation in 1986. With far less caution, he sent troops into the townships to clamp down on anti-apartheid activities.

1986 was the tenth anniversary of the Soweto uprising. The government, fearing that the situation would become explosive, unsuccessfully made a last-minute attempt to prohibit a planned stayaway on 16 June. Instead, Botha imposed the most repressive State of Emergency ever in the country's history and thousands of activists were detained without trial. As was to become common practice, many political activists were viciously interrogated and brutally tortured.

When Archbishop Desmond Tutu called for further international sanctions against South Africa in October 1986, Botha responded characteristically: *'South Africa is not a jellyfish and is in many respects a swordfish.'* Still wanting to appear invulnerable, Botha was defiant in the face of sanctions and gave no indication of the secret meetings his officials were having with Mandela.

Disenchanted white academics, politicians and businessmen began to make pilgrimages to the ANC in exile. The largest of these meetings was held in Dakar where some 61 mainly Afrikaans-speaking South Africans met with an ANC delegation in July 1987. The Dakar Safari, as it became known, organised by the Institute for Democracy in South Africa (Idasa), was a political watershed. All those around the table agreed to the need for negotiations, the release of political prisoners and the unbanning of the ANC. Although the NIS tacitly supported the meeting, President Botha was furious and accused the South African delegation of legitimising 'terrorists'.

3

# 'Walk through the open door ...'

2 February
1990

One month after De Klerk had replaced the ailing PW Botha as State President, he unconditionally released seven political prisoners from prison. Although this was a positive indication that the government was prepared to go some way in meeting the demands of the Declaration, nobody knew how far he would go.

At the Opening of Parliament on 2 February 1990, people packed the public gallery and hordes of press waited expectantly. They were hoping to hear that Nelson Mandela would be released that day. However, De Klerk – and in fact Mandela himself – felt his release would overshadow the more extensive changes De Klerk was about to announce.

De Klerk opened his historic speech – and the door to constitutional negotiations – by saying, 'The general election on 6 September 1989 placed our country irrevocably on the road of drastic change. Underlying this is the growing realisation by an increasing number of South Africans that only a negotiated understanding among the representative leaders of the entire population can ensure lasting peace.' De Klerk went on to meet most of the conditions stipulated in the Harare Declaration, announcing the unbanning of the ANC, the PAC and the South African Communist Party; the lifting of the State of Emergency; the immediate release of all political prisoners; the unconditional return of exiles; and the freedom for trade unions to function openly. He ended his speech with a broad invitation to all organisations to 'Walk through the open door and take your place at the negotiating table'.

The country, indeed the whole world, was stunned. Archbishop Desmond Tutu expressed the surprise of most when he said, 'He has taken my breath away.'

'I didn't want this leaked to the press, so I made them promise, because usually they do leak, not even to talk to their wives, and I promised not to tell my wife, and for once we kept the secret because we wanted maximum impact of the announcement so that we could change the whole attitude of South Africans and the rest of the world to see that this was serious and we were not playing games. On the way to Parliament I said to my wife, "South Africa will never be the same again." and she understood.' – FW de Klerk

Although De Klerk did not release Mandela on that day, he did make a public commitment to do so.

**1** Celebrations in the streets of Johannesburg following the unbanning of the ANC, 1990.
© Graeme Williams

**2** A man holds up the good news for all to see, 1990. © Benny Gool / Oryx Archives

# Negotiating One Law for One Nation

# 1990 - 1994

'The formal negotiations process which began with the first face-to-face meeting of the apartheid government and the ANC at Groote Schuur in Cape Town in 1990 was the climax of over a century of engagement between black and white South Africans which had taken many different forms. It was the remarkable confluence of a number of global, regional and national factors which enabled these two sworn enemies to sit down at the same table to discuss the country's future.'

Cyril Ramaphosa, Chairperson of the Constitutional Assembly

1

'The majority of South Africans, black and white, recognise that apartheid has no future. ... Our march to freedom is irreversible. We must not allow fear to stand in our way. Universal suffrage on a common voters' roll in a united, democratic and non-racial South Africa is the only way to racial harmony.'

'I have discovered the secret that after climbing a great hill, one only finds that there are many more hills to climb ... I can rest only for a moment ... I dare not linger, for my long walk is not yet ended. If you want to make peace with your enemy, you have to work with your enemy. Then he becomes your partner.'

In his autobiography *Long Walk to Freedom* Mandela warned South Africans that the test of their 'devotion to freedom' was just beginning and that there was a long road ahead:

**1** Nelson Mandela travelling to the Grand Parade in Cape Town, directly after his release, February 1990. © *Avusa*

**2** A crowd surrounding Nelson Mandela's motorcade, Cape Town, February 1990. © *Elmond Jiyane*

**3** Thousands gather at Jabulani Stadium for the ANC rally to welcome home Nelson Mandela to Soweto. © *Robert Botha / Business Day*

**4** Nelson Mandela's first public address directly after his release from prison, at the Grand Parade, Cape Town, 11 February 1990. © *Rashid Lombard*

4

# Conditions for negotiations

**February 1990**

Mandela's words were prophetic. From the time of his release, it took nearly two years for real negotiations between the political parties to get underway and six years for the settlement of a final constitution. Leon Wessels, one of the NP's chief negotiators, later reflected: *'Few people would have forecast at the time that it would take another tortuous journey along seemingly impassable roads before South Africa's new Constitution could be finally signed.'*

The NP and the ANC first had to discuss the conditions under which they would negotiate with each other. Both faced many challenges. For a start, the ANC had to transform itself overnight from a liberation movement into a political party and set up the internal machinery to sustain the negotiations.

*'The ANC has just been unbanned after operating illegally for 30 years and engaging in largely clandestine activities. If it is to succeed in carrying the majority of people along with it, we need to have visible branches in every locality and in every neighbourhood where ordinary people can participate in its decision-making,'* explained Valli Moosa, who was later to become a key figure in the constitution-making process. It was in these branches that leaders hoped to

persuade their followers that a negotiated settlement, as opposed to a more decisive revolutionary victory, was the right path to follow. They also had to ensure that the comrades who had been fighting in the trenches viewed negotiations as 'the new terrain of struggle' rather than as a form of 'selling out' to the enemy. In its negotiations with the NP, the ANC fought to 'level the playing field', a phrase that was to recur often, insisting on the immediate release of all political prisoners and the return of all political exiles as a basic requirement for establishing the 'right climate of negotiations'.

De Klerk, on the other hand, faced the task of maintaining unity in his party and bringing the white community with him to the negotiating table. Tertius Delport, a key NP roleplayer, expressed what he saw as the fears of the party's constituency at the time: *'The ANC are going to take our land. They're going to take everything that we've worked for. We're going to have no law and order. It won't be safe to walk the streets. The SACP and MK [Umkhonto we Sizwe] want an absolute domination in a one-party state and we will have a totally socialist approach to the economy … the NP desperately has to fight for minority protection so that one group or party cannot grab all the power. We have to ensure a multi-party situation in South Africa.'*

1

**1** Alfred Nzo and Joe Slovo return to South Africa after years in exile. They are met at DF Malan Airport by their friend and comrade, Nelson Mandela, April 1990. © Benny Gool / Oryx Archives

**2** 'For us who have suffered the curse of exile for close to 30 years this is a moment of the greatest joy … We are at last back in this beautiful country and among people we love. But it is also a moment of sadness because there lie buried in our soil some of the finest sons and daughters of our nation.' Joe Slovo General-Secretary of the SACP, 29 April 1990. © Elmond Jiyane

**3** In 1990, Ruth Mompati, Joe Slovo, Alfred Nzo, Joe Modise and Thabo Mbeki returned to South Africa to form part of the ANC team that met with the National Party government, Cape Town, 1990. © Gallo Images / Media24

# Violence flares

Besides ensuring minority protection in any future settlement, De Klerk also had to persuade the security forces to redefine their role and adapt to the new circumstances in the country. Up to this point, they had been given free range to conduct a no-holds-barred campaign against the ANC and other liberation movements that had been barred.

The security situation in the country was complicated, however, by the intense violence that had flared up in townships across the country since Mandela's release. Seven hundred people died in the first eight months of 1990. The violence was at its worst in the industrial townships in the province of the Transvaal and in Natal where the ANC, the IFP and the security forces were locked in a bloody battle. There was also widespread instability in the 'homelands' of Bophuthatswana, Gazankulu, Venda, the Transkei and the Ciskei, with most of the populace demanding to be reincorporated back into South Africa.

The first official 'talks about talks' that were set to take place on 11 April 1990 were cancelled when the ANC accused the police of the 'unprovoked killing and maiming of defenceless demonstrators' in Sebokeng,

just south of Johannesburg. Twelve people were killed and many more hundreds were injured. Mandela asked De Klerk how he could 'talk about negotiations on one hand and murder our people on the other'. De Klerk vehemently denied this accusation and supported the police claim that they had been 'attacked by an unruly mob'. The peace process teetered. Eventually De Klerk agreed to appoint an independent commission of inquiry to investigate the massacre. Talks were rescheduled for 2 May 1990.

The Goldstone Commission later found the police responsible for the Sebokeng shootings. As a conciliatory gesture, De Klerk granted indemnity to all ANC exiles who were to be involved in the talks with the government. Thabo Mbeki, Joe Slovo, Joe Modise, Alfred Nzo and Ruth Mompati flew home from Lusaka. Crowds of jubilant ANC supporters waited at Cape Town airport to greet them. These stalwarts of the struggle who had lived in exile for so many years were finally unbanned and had the right to speak in South Africa without risking prosecution. Mbeki later wondered *'why people had to wait for so many years and so many people dead to do something as easy as what we are doing … to come back.'*

2

3

# Groote Schuur

On 2 May 1990, the NP and the ANC began a two-day series of 'talks about talks' at the historic Groote Schuur homestead in Cape Town. It was at this grand former residence of South African heads of government that the two parties sat across a large dining-room table and identified the obstacles to negotiations and ways of overcoming them. The meeting was very tense – both sides were highly suspicious of each other. As Roelf Meyer later described it, 'it was as though people from the two polar regions were meeting for the first time':

*'The government delegation felt unsure because nobody knew what to expect. We had to sit across the table from enemies of long standing, and they were total strangers to us. What kind of people were they? What would happen? It reminded me of my first flight in a jet fighter. On the one hand I was filled with uncertainty, but on the other hand it was an unbelievable injection of adrenalin.'*

According to Thabo Mbeki, it took only a few minutes before 'everyone understood that there was no one in the room that had horns' and they soon got down to the points on the agenda. This included the drawing up of a timetable for the release of political prisoners and the granting of immunity from prosecution for politically motivated offences so that exiled members of the ANC could return to the country. The two parties also discussed the State of Emergency, the presence of troops in the township and ways of stemming the violence.

During this meeting, the ANC refused to accede to the NP's key demand to disband MK. De Klerk needed this concession to allay fears in the white community. Although the NP had made important shifts, it still saw the protection of white 'group' interests as its core mission and wanted to keep tight control over the process of transition. Neither party, however, had a clear plan as to how it would proceed. They found themselves on uncharted waters and both, on reflection, saw the need to remain as flexible and open as possible.

The meeting ended with what De Klerk and Mandela described as a 'broad agreement' between the parties, in the form of the historic Groote Schuur Minute. The two men stood together in front of a bank of cameras to announce their commitment to a new order in South Africa. Mandela declared: *'Not only are we closer to one another, the ANC and the government, but we are all victors. South Africa is the victor.'*

De Klerk later recalled, *'Mandela and I shook hands and the message was sent to the world that the first step to a negotiated settlement had been successfully taken. It would, however, take far longer than I had hoped to complete the second step.'*

1

**1** Nelson Mandela walking with FW de Klerk and Minister of Foreign Affairs, Pik Botha, to sign the Groote Schuur Minute, 5 May 1990. © *Benny Gool / Oryx Archives*

**2** Nelson Mandela and FW de Klerk address the media following breakthrough talks at Groote Schuur, Cape Town, 5 May 1990. © *Benny Gool / Oryx Archives*

**3** Media from across the globe capture this historic event. © *Benny Gool / Oryx Archives*

2

3

# People's power

While it appeared that a new era of free political activity was emerging, the reality on the ground was far more complex. Apartheid legislation may have been scrapped but the institutions of apartheid – the police, the civil service and the judiciary – were still firmly in place. Most South Africans still did not have the right to vote. Moreover, the legacy of apartheid would take a long time to disappear. As Cheryl Carolus, a member of the ANC negotiating team, said at the time:

'The battery of laws that have been in existence until now said that anybody who differs from the government can be jailed. They legislated political intolerance. People today still cannot understand that I can stand up today and have one view and Chris Hani can stand up tomorrow and have a completely different view and we're all in the same organisation because people don't understand political tolerance. That will take a long time to overcome.'

**1** Protestors calling for change, Cape Town, November 1990. © *Adil Bradlow / Oryx Archives*

**2** A public call for the release of all political prisoners, Cape Town, 1990. © *Adil Bradow / Oryx Archives*

1

The ANC for its part sought more rapid and radical transformation, as expressed in its 1991 slogan, 'Mass Action for the Transfer of Power to the People'. Young ANC comrades were in particular growing restless and angry at what they perceived as the government's lack of commitment to fundamental change. They believed it was a tactical error for the ANC to have suspended the armed struggle and trusted De Klerk.

While Mandela reiterated the ANC's support for negotiations, party leaders began to push for the acceleration of change.

*'We need mass pressure specifically for the purposes of forcing the government to move along, implement the Pretoria Minute and bring about change at a faster pace. We need that exertion of people's power.'* - Valli Moosa.

Just a month after the opening of Parliament, Mandela underscored the growing ill will between the government and the ANC: *'There is no meeting of the minds between us and the government on the real meaning of democracy. There will be no discussions on the constitution until all obstacles are removed.'*

# Blood on the tracks

23 February
1991

The greatest obstacle to negotiations remained the wave upon wave of violence that had engulfed the country. Between 1991 and 1992, over 6 000 people lost their lives in the gruesome township wars. Political parties blamed each other and made little headway in putting a stop to the carnage, despite multiple initiatives by various leaders. After his release Nelson Mandela had famously appealed to ANC supporters at a large rally in Durban:

'My message to those of you involved in this battle of brother against brother is this: Take your guns, your knives and your pangas and throw them into the sea … We commend Inkatha for their demand over the years for the unbanning of the ANC and the release of political prisoners, as well as for their stand for refusing to participate in a negotiated settlement without the creation of a necessary climate … We recognise that in order to bring the war to an end, the two sides must talk.'

Analysts struggled to make sense of the bloodbath that ensued and put forward explanations ranging from the legacy of apartheid to the ANC's campaign of ungovernability and rivalry between the ANC and Inkatha for political supremacy. While these arguments abounded, the ongoing cycle of violence severely eroded trust between the parties.

**1** An IFP demonstration, February 1994. © *Adil Bradlow / Oryx Archives*

**2** ANC march. © *Paul Weinberg / Africa Media Online*

**3** Guns became rife in clashes in the townships. © *Source unknown*

**4** A violent demonstration against the homeland government in Garankuwa, Bophuthatswana, 1990. © *Graeme Williams*

**5** A victim thrown from a train in Soweto during the period of train violence, 1990. © *Graeme Williams*

1

Development, spoke of the impossibility of handing power to 'an unsophisticated majority' who were 'not used to political power' and who did not have 'the expertise of running a country'.

Cheryl Carolus expressed the ANC's sense of collective outrage at the NP's position on this matter: *'The NP see themselves as in the driving seat, as retaining full control of the steering wheel through this whole process and arriving fairly intact on the other side. We are absolutely adamant that we want an all-party conference to decide on how an interim government makes transitional arrangements and about the basic principles of a constitution without making any guarantees to the NP. The issues are all negotiable. What is non-negotiable for us is that nobody can be player and referee and take the gate takings.'*

Others in the NP cabinet were even more emphatic in their objections to the idea of an interim government. Tertius Delport declared: 'We're not an illegal government. We are here as a result of a historical fact. And whatever is going to happen will be because we say so.' Gerrit Viljoen, the Minister of Constitutional

2

# The National Peace Accord

## September 1991

A major breakthrough came with the signing of the National Peace Accord. This document was the result of the first multi-party conference on South African soil, organised with the assistance of churches and business leaders. Roelf Meyer described the Peace Accord 'as having provided the best possible chance to find ways to stop violence'. It also provided a solid basis for the negotiations that lay ahead:

*'Up to that stage we had not negotiated; we had simply talked. The Peace Conference offered a learning opportunity which came in handy in the negotiations which were to follow.'*

The signing of the Accord was followed by the launch of the Patriotic Front (PF), a loose alliance of some 92 organisations that had opposed apartheid. The establishment of the PF ultimately changed the political balance of forces in favour of the ANC. At its inaugural conference, the PF issued a declaration that included three important principles for the negotiated transfer of power. The first was that an interim government had to oversee the process of democratising South Africa as the present government lacked legitimacy. The second was that only a constitutional assembly, elected on a one-person one-vote basis in a united South Africa could draft and adopt a democratic constitution. The last was that

**1** IFP members march through the city of Johannesburg during the time of the signing of the Peace Accord, 1991. © *Graeme Williams*

**2** Cosatu march, Cape Town, 1992. © *Adil Bradlow / Oryx Archive*

1

an all-party congress should be held as soon as possible. Although there was little doubt that the ANC and the NP were the two major contenders for power in the country, the ANC strongly believed that the negotiations would not work if a deal was simply hammered out between the two. As Mac Maharaj commented:

*'In advocating a multi-party process Nelson Mandela was saying, "Take on board everybody, whether they are apartheid puppets or not so that we get the maximum unity."'*

Weeks of hard bargaining in bilateral and multilateral meetings followed. Suspicions between the parties remained rife. The more hard-line faction in the NP believed that the ANC was in the thrall of both the SACP and the Congress of South African Trade Unions (Cosatu) and that these organisations were still hoping for 'a radical seizure of power'. Tertius Delport, who was initially a central negotiator for the NP, declared:

*'The whole idea of a take-over still isn't dead in the ranks of the ANC. I have my doubts whether the ANC as an organisation isn't merely seen by the communists as a vehicle to get there,'*

2

# The end of talking, the start of negotiations

## November 1991

In late November 1991, the second All-Party Preparatory Meeting gathered to plan for a permanent negotiating forum, the Convention for a Democratic South Africa (Codesa). At the preparatory meeting, delegates from all over the country chose the World Trade Centre in Kempton Park as Codesa's home. This rather drab and unimaginative locale was to become the backdrop for some of the most important and lively events in South Africa's history. It was here that constitution-making would take place.

One of the most difficult issues was how decisions would be made at Codesa. *'At that time, the self-confidence and assumed superiority of those who had been in charge was very pronounced. We had to fight hard and insistently to get points accepted,'* commented Albie Sachs who had recently returned from exile.

The ANC believed that decisions at Codesa should not be made by a 'yea or nay' or the counting of hands, and opposed the idea that each of the parties present could have an equal vote. The government and other, smaller parties ultimately agreed to the principle of 'sufficient consensus' for coming to decisions. This turned out to be a very creative solution. Only the IFP felt aggrieved by this arrangement. It was decided that two independent persons who were not part of the negotiation process should be given the responsibility of deciding whether consensus had been achieved or not. Two judges of the Supreme Court, Piet Schabort and Ismail Mohammed, were chosen to preside over Codesa. The NP also agreed that Codesa decisions would be binding on the government and all parties. Parliament would be asked to give legal force to the agreements so as to uphold its legitimacy.

1

## CODESA
### Convention for a Democratic South Africa

PO Box 307 ISANDO 1600 South Africa ** Telephone (011) 397-1198/99 Fax (011) 397-2211

9 December 1991

To: Conservative Party of South Africa
P.O. Box 1642 Pretoria 0001
Fax: (012) 21-5270

CONVENTION FOR A DEMOCRATIC SOUTH AFRICA

The Steering Committee established by the Preparatory Meeting of the Convention for a Democratic South Africa (CODESA) hereby extends to your organisation an invitation to attend the first meeting of CODESA, which will take place at the World Trade Centre near Jan Smuts Airport on 20 and 21 December 1991.

Each participating organisation has been allocated a maximum of 12 delegates.

We shall be pleased to receive at your earliest convenience the number and names of the delegates that will be representing your organisation at CODESA. For your convenience, the details for communication and on-going contact with the Steering Committee appear above.

We also attach herewith a summary of the decisions of the Preparatory Meeting for your information.

Yours faithfully

*J. Mahomed*

JUSTICE P.J. SCHABORT AND JUSTICE ISMAIL MAHOMED
CO-CHAIRPERSONS STEERING COMMITTEE OF CODESA

2

## African National Congress

51 Plein Street
Johannesburg 2001
P O Box 61884
Marshalltown 2107

Tel: (011) 330-70
Fax: (011) 330-90
Telex: 4212

18 December 1991

The Administration Office
CODESA
c/o World Trade Centre
ISANDO

Dear Sir/Madam

In response to your request for lists of our delegates, advisors and support staff, below is a list of our support staff:

Gill Marcus
Karl Niehaus
Sakkie Macozoma
Jessie Duarte
Annalise Anderson
Sbongile Mahlangu
Ricky Nkondo
Andile Ngcaba
Lindi Sisulu-Guma

We hope that this will suffice.

Yours sincerely

pp:
M C Ramaphosa
SECRETARY GENERAL

MCR/sm

## Public Media Observations on Codesa

End of first day of Codesa shattered atmosphere of bonhomie that had been created and marked the start of "real" negotiations.

Codesa will survive battle. But last night's battle showed that the Gov't is going to fight hard and close to dirty — and the ANC will lash out equally viciously if it feels it is being like a piccanin. Gov't put ANC on the spot with its out-of-the-blue proposal for far-reaching short-term changes to the structure of Parliament and the executive — Star editorial 21/12/91

∧ ∧ ∧

The IFP is raising quibbles at every available opportunity.

_Codesa was even prepared to offer the King an opportunity to address the meeting_

It is fair to entertain that the party might be seeking to raise its profile in the multi party process by raising unnecessary objections. It is fair to say that people

who want a peaceful solution as soon as possible are sick and tired of quibbling which frustrates that aim. Star editorial 23.12.91

∧ ∧ ∧

Tracas was something much deeper that a disagreement over status of MK & Pretoria minute. It was a warning from black SA. to white SA.

Friday 20/12 marks the moment at which black SA came of political age. It did so on its own terms.

De Klerk made a fundamental error. He used the final speaking opportunity, granted to him magnanimously by the ANC., to hector and threaten the ANC in the tones of a head master admonishing an errant child.

Many present who found it distasteful, felt that he had overstepped bounds of political debate, that he became too personal in his attack but Mr M's anger was genuine.

2

---

**1** Nelson Mandela and FW de Klerk in an angry exchange just before the end of the opening session of Codesa. © Graeme Williams

**2** Notes taken by Nelson Mandela on the media coverage of the heated exchange between him and De Klerk. © Nelson Mandela Centre of Memory

# A giant leap forward

'Codesa has made a giant leap forward from the days of an apartheid South Africa. Future South Africans will identify this day and this moment as the time when South Africa was reborn. No one believes that the journey will be easy but it is a journey we must take.'
- Justice Ismail Mohammed

'Our date with destiny has arrived. Never mind that Codesa is clumsily named, oddly located and subject to fits of pique by its participants – it is a moment of truth. There is an evocative Zulu phrase to describe this moment: "asijiki", no turning back. - *The Star*

'Any attempts by Codesa to enforce its illegitimate discussions or actions will be considered an act of war … If ever the peace-loving and law-abiding Boers were to be aroused into resistance and total rejection of this renegade government, we have now arrived at the moment in our history.'
- Afrikaner Weerstandsbeweging (AWB)

'Today the race for a truly democratic South Africa has reached the home straight when sworn enemies are walking the last mile in a spirit of national reconciliation to reach the winning post of a truly non-racial South Africa free of the shackles of the past. Our only regret is that there are empty chairs. We must mediate so the chairs can be filled.'
- Amichand Rajbansi, National People's Party

'The birth of Codesa gave tremendous impetus. We succeeded in bringing most of the parties together and getting them to be committed. A kind of atmosphere started to grow in South Africa, emphasising negotiation as opposed to an armed solution. The world was quite amazed that that was what we could do. They thought these Boers are too stupid and the ANC is too belligerent and they couldn't understand this coming together. And from this grew at least the beginning of nationhood.'
- Kobie Coetsee, Minister of Justice and member of the NP negotiating team

'The ANC message at Codesa is clear and straightforward – the time for one South Africa, one nation, one vote, one future is here.'
- Nelson Mandela

**1** A cartoon by Zapiro printed in *Negotiation News*, 24 April 1992. © Zapiro

**2** ANC stalwarts Albertina Sisulu, Adelaide Tambo and Rica Hodgson with a group of women, protesting for better representation of women at Codesa. © Robert Botha

# Protests Outside the World Trade Centre

At the start of the negotiation process, a wide range of women's organisations felt that women were inadequately represented at the negotiating table. The ANC Women's League galvanised an extremely heterogeneous grouping of South African women to fight for women's inclusion. The Women's National Coalition (WNC) became a very vocal and important advocacy group. Joyce Seroke, a member of the Coalition, tells how groups of women,

*'would wait for strategic opportunities to chant freedom songs and parade banners voicing our demands. We would also ensure that there were deliberately vacant seats in the main hall denoting the absence of women. These were exciting moments, with a strong sense of unity and common purpose amongst very diverse women's groupings.'*

2

# Giving and taking

## 6 February 1992

The Codesa Management Committee had the Herculean task of keeping 19 political parties happy while driving the process forward. It set up five working groups to produce agreements for presentation to a plenary by the end of March 1992. They were: **Working Group 1** to create a climate for free political participation; **Working Group 2** to draft general constitutional principles and decide on the most acceptable constitution-making body; **Working Group 3** to agree on transitional arrangements or an interim government; **Working Group 4** to decide on the constitutional future of the 'TBVC' [Transkei, Bophuthatswana, Venda, Ciskei] homelands; **Working Group 5** to set target dates for decisions and their implementation.

President De Klerk declared: *'Success or failure of the working groups will be determined very largely by the will of the delegates to find one another by means of giving and taking.'*

1

Republiek van Suid-Afrika    Republic of South Africa

Ministerie van Staatkundige Ontwikkeling
Ministry of Constitutional Development

Verwysing          3-A5/6/12                    Privaatsak
Reference                                        Private Bag
                                                 Pretoria
                                                 0001
                                                 1992-01-12

The Secretariat: CODESA
P O Box 307
ISANDO
1400

Dear Sir

ADVISORS TO THE SA GOVERNMENT'S DELEGATION

By direction of Dr G van N Viljoen the following persons are hereby nominated as advisors to the SA Government's delegation at the five CODESA working groups:

Working Group 1:  Dr L D Barnard
                  Mr D C D Swanepoel

Working Group 2:  Dr F Venter
                  Mr G H Grové

Working Group 3:  Mr J J Noëth
                  Dr G C von Bratt

Working Group 4:  Mr N P van Heerden
                  Mr G P Croeser

Working Group 5:  Dr H P Fourie
                  Mr J M Spaarwater

Yours sincerely

PRIVATE SECRETARY

2

C·O·D·E·S·A

TO       :   MEMBERS OF WORKING GROUP 2,
             COORDINATORS OF WORKING GROUP 2

FROM     :   CODESA ADMINISTRATION

QUERIES  :   LOVEDALIA OR DIANNE

RE       :   WG2 DRAFT MINUTES FOR 11/2 AND
             DRAFT AGENDA FOR 17/2

PLEASE NOTIFY US IMMEDIATELY IF YOUR FAX NUMBER OR ADDRESS HAS CHANGED. WE CANNOT BE HELD RESPONSIBLE FOR ENSURING THAT YOU RECEIVE COPIES OF ALL DOCUMENTATION UNLESS WE ARE KEPT INFORMED OF THESE CHANGES.

WORKING GROUP 2

ANC
Negotiation Comm         (011) 333-9090
C Ramaphosa              (011) 29-0097
M V Moosa                (011) 333-9090
F Ginwala                (011) 333-7739
A Sachs                  (021) 22-2626

BOPHUTHATSWANA GOVERNMENT
D Schoeman               (0140) 84-2943
S G Mothibe              (0140) 84-2406
R Cronje                 (0140) 84-2733
T E Scheepers            (0140) 24618
I Findlay                (0140) 84-2733

CISKEI GOVERNMENT
H J S Kayser             (0401) 91189
M C Kashe                (0401) 95-1165
I J Smuts                (0461) 29664
J Labuschagne            (04634) 31902
V R Zietsman

DEMOCRATIC PARTY
C W Eglin                (021) 461-0092
D Worrall                (021) 461-0092
A J Leon                 (021) 461-0092
D Welsh                  (021) 461-0092

DIKWANKWETLA PARTY
S O M Moji               (01438) 31218
M M Makhalemele
S K Mopeli
M Mopeli                 (01438) 36306

IFP
S Felgate                (0358) 20-2167
A P Blaustein            (091) 609-757-6487
S H Gumede               (0358) 20-2430
M Alachouzos
B S Ngubane              (0358) 20-2469

INTANDO YESIZWE PARTY
J S Mabona               (01215) 2548
S J Mgidi                (01215) 2808
A P Laka                 (01215) 2808
M P Mahlangu             (01215) 2808
I T Mahlangu             (01215) 2808

INYANDZA NATIONAL MOVEMENT
E N Ginindza             (01314) 72184
C Albertyn               (031) 23-1638 (M)
I B Lephoko              (01314) 72184
B E Mabuza               (01314) 72184

LABOUR PARTY OF SA
I M Richards             (021) 45-1953
D Lockey
M Hendrickse             (0422) 922-3156
C I Nasson

NIC/TIC
P G Gordhan              (031) 309-2278
N Pillay                 (012) 374-4792
N Haysom                 (011) 403-1764
F Cachalia
Z Yacoob
I C Meer

NATIONAL PARTY
F J van Heerden          (021) 461-5329
J A Rabie                (021) 403-3507
S Camerer                (021) 461-5329 or (011) 838-6262
I M Rautenbach           (011) 489-2049

NATIONAL PEOPLE'S PARTY
M M Mohanlall            (021) 403-2971 (M)
S Ismail                 (011) 331-2970
B Singh                  (0331) 91-2015
H M Meerahoo             (0331) 91-2015

SOLIDARITY PARTY
I Omar                   (0331) 42-7368 or 92-2171
D S Rajah                (0331) 42-7368
K Reddy                  (011) 333-0981
R Arenstein              (031) 304-7009

SA COMMUNIST PARTY
G Fraser-Moleketi        (011) 836-8366
B Nzimande               (0331) 95-5599
J Slovo                  (011) 836-8366
N Hoosain                (041) 54-4233
E Daniels                (021) 761-8515

CONVENTION FOR A DEMOCRATIC SOUTH AFRICA

PO Box 307, Isando, 1600, South Africa.
Telephone (011) 397-1196/99. Fax (011) 397-2221

# Deadlock

The percentage issue clouded much bigger differences. What was at stake was the basic system of governance. The ANC could not accept what Joe Slovo described as the government's 'loser takes all' proposals for a multi-person presidency that would rotate among incumbents, a three-party executive that could veto decisions and special representation of minority parties in the upper house. The ANC remained intent on one-person one-vote, a majority government and no special veto powers for the minority parties. For Valli Moosa, co-convener of Working Group 2, this moment showed 'the world that the NP does not want to subject itself to the will of the majority'. Mandela concurred:

*'The NP mouth acceptance of one-person one-vote, but then propose a constitutional dispensation that makes provisions to ignore the verdict of the electorate.'*

Ramaphosa then announced that the ANC was withdrawing from Working Group 2. 'We needed to underpin whatever we did by continuous common understanding and we didn't have it,' he said. In Albie Sachs's view, *'Looking back now on that whole period we were making all the concessions towards the end and they weren't meeting us. They weren't looking for a way out. It was clear they wanted a deadlock.'*

For its part, the NP accused the ANC of bullying tactics. Roelf Meyer believed that *'Ramaphosa was forced to call for a deadlock in Codesa. I would rather put the blame on the other side.'* An NP document from the time stated that *'An honest analysis of the events leading to the present impasse makes it clear that the ANC is responsible for obstructing the negotiation process … The ANC's perception, it would seem, was that its purpose of an unqualified take-over of power would not be served by the reasonable agreements in Codesa that were ready to be sealed.'*

The ANC's withdrawal marked the end of the Codesa phase of the negotiations. The country was still a long way off from a negotiated settlement.

1

**Statement by the Secretary Genaral of the African National Congress - 14 May, 1992**

We are not surprised at the National Party's stubborn and greedy line on the question on the question of decision-making. They are used to making all decisions by themselves and treating the county as if it belonged to them alone, and as if no real changes were taking place. In this week when even their own supporters are shattered by revelations of their corruption and cruelty, they have the effrontery to offer us lessons in democracy. Their so-called compromise proposals have jumped around from one hour to the next, usually getting worse rather than better each time. Long after the idea had been accepted that the Senate should be involved in the legislative process only, and not in the constitution-making process, the government attempts to lumber the negotiations with the clumsy idea of a Senate veto. The final proposals they put on the table were considerably worse than the what they had agreed to yesterday. They are either very clumsy or else playing around with what should be serious matters.

The ANC without any prompting put forward the proposal that the Bill of Rights be adopted by a majority of 75%. This was not a bargaining chip. We are not dealing with the price of a second hand motor car. The Bill of Rights touches on the most fundamental values of our society. It recognises the dream of all our people to live in freedom, equality and security. It protects language, cultural and religious rights.

We regard these aspects as so fundamental that we felt they should receive the assent of at least three quarters of the delegates at the National Assembly.

We also supported the proposal for special regional representation in the National Assembly and a special majority of regional representatives for issues directly affecting the regions. For the rest we have stood by the two thirds majority that worked so well in Namibia that in the end their Constitution was adopted unanimously.

We are firmly embarked on the course of democracy. There can be no turning back and no delays.

Cyril Ramaphosa
Secretary General

**1** Statement signed by ANC Secretary-General Cyril Ramaphosa at the time of the ANC's withdrawal from the negotiations, 14 May 1992. © *UWC / Robben Island Museum / Mayibuye Archives*

1

# Stage Two: Multi-party negotiations
May 1992 - April 1994

## 'An autumn of despair'

The collapse of Codesa was a moment of crisis in the negotiating process. Dr Zach de Beer, leader of the Democratic Party (DP) and the first chair of the Codesa Management Committee, expressed his regret that 'the spirit of Codesa' seemed to have evaporated. *'It was very sad that there was a great deal of public recrimination between two very important organisations in the sight of all of the world. We are ill served by these events ... I hope the spirit of Codesa is coming back into our hearts.'*

The spirit did not return. Accusation followed counter-accusation and by the autumn of 1992 despair had set in. Political violence was worse than ever and people were being killed daily in political clashes. Mandela repeatedly voiced his disbelief that a head of state, with a sophisticated security apparatus, could not do something to stop the violence. In his address to the OAU in April 1992, he did not mince his words:

**1** Archbishop Desmond Tutu speaking at a funeral. © *Graeme Williams / Africa Media online*

**2** A crowd of angry residents at a protest march. Alexandra, 26 March 1992. © *Sowatan /Avusa*

*'The situation is increasingly comparable with that of Nazi Germany where people were killed only because they were Jews. In today's "apartheid-free" South Africa, our people are massacred simply because they are black. White indifference is appalling ... Pretoria's propaganda machine has put across the image that this violence is a result of a political power struggle between various black organisations. When the ANC first spoke of a Third Force, it was laughed out of court. Yet today, with over 13 000 lives lost, this concept has been recognised by most commentators within South Africa ... The partiality of the police, the lack of arrest or conviction, confirm mounting evidence that the violence erupts at points which most weaken the ANC.'*

At this point, the IFP agreed that not enough was being done to halt the violence. The party's Suzanne Vos commented: *'Inkatha have been hard hit by the violence. More than a dozen of our local leadership and some of our senior leadership ... have been assassinated or badly wounded. Not enough arrests are being made.'*

But NP's Sheila Camerer defended the police: *'It's easy to blame the police ... I think the police have a ghastly time of it trying to keep peace in the townships. They're put in an impossible position most of the time. They're shot at. A lot of them have been killed. What police force in the world is killed off like they are?'*

In response to the stalemate, Mandela laid out concrete and achievable conditions for the resumption of negotiations. A primary condition was the establishment of an interim government. Valli Moosa explained: *'White minority rule and violence are two sides of the same coin. However much we may cry out against the violence and demand that the government stops it, they will be involved. For that reason, it is urgent to establish an interim government of national unity and also to have democratic elections to change the balance of forces.'*

# Rolling mass action

June
1992

While the politicians battled it out, the grassroots members of the ANC/SACP/Cosatu Alliance felt increasingly frustrated and disappointed. For most people in townships across the country, there were no visible changes. How people lived, how laws were made, who ran the police and army, who owned the land, were all exactly as before. Moreover, their lives were now plagued by violence. The language of politics became increasingly hostile and confrontational.

The NP's Dawie de Villiers, concerned that 'this kind of war talk only increased the levels of violence', pleaded that 'leaders on all sides start talking in conciliatory terms'. But the ANC/SACP/Cosatu Alliance decided to demonstrate its power through the use of 'rolling mass action', in the hope that strikes and street demonstrations would force the NP to agree to an interim government.

The first stayaway took place symbolically on 16 June, the day that students in Soweto had risen up against the enforced use of Afrikaans in the schools 16 years previously. Ramaphosa reflected on the importance of this tactic for the ANC:

*'The breaking off of talks marked an important return for the ANC to the politics of mass mobilisation. It served to remind the illegitimate regime that they were negotiating with a political movement which had the support of the majority of South Africans.'*

The NP reacted with fury to what they believed was 'euphemistically called mass action but was in reality, physical confrontation'. The party believed that the ANC was 'now making demands in a threatening manner in order to coerce the Government into irresponsible concessions that could not be negotiated with the parties at Codesa'. The NP was certain that this climate of 'militant thinking' was created by the undue influence of a 'cabal' in the ANC with close links to Cosatu and the SACP, which 'undermined the attempts of many ANC realists to negotiate in good faith'. Tertius Delport remarked: '

*The radicals have taken over. There's no hope of negotiations succeeding whilst this insurrectionist school are in command. We're dealing with people who are only committed to grabbing all of the state power in this country. We've been bending backwards to accommodate them whilst they have been at us hammer and tongs to discredit us. Those days are over. We've also got a constituency.'*

More diplomatically, Roelf Meyer declared, 'Ultimatum politics can't be part of the negotiation process.' The NP concluded that the ANC 'simply do not seem able to adjust to a democratic political process ... ANC rhetoric has degenerated into incitement to violence and hatred at grassroots level.'

1 Placard accusing FW de Klerk of being a murderer during the Defend Democracy campaign in Cape Town. © Benny Gool / Oryx Archives

2 Comrades protesting in Alexandra. © Graeme Williams

*'From the disaster of the deadlock there grew a situation of mutual trust between the ANC and us. Such a situation did not exist at Codesa 2 … To my mind the period July-September 1992 was the most crucial time in the whole negotiating process … Our view became that there was no problem that we could not resolve. It almost became a slogan in the negotiations and a strong motivation for the settling of disputes,'* comments Roelf Meyer.

For Leon Wessels, then Deputy Minister of Foreign Affairs, Ramaphosa's and Meyer's similar style of 'never being prepared to accept defeat and always searching for mutually acceptable answers' was an important ingredient in the final success of the negotiations. It allowed the ANC and the NP to remain close to each other in respect of the process even when there were major differences on policy matters.

Some commentators have portrayed Ramaphosa as having a 'psychological advantage' over his negotiating partner and Meyer as constantly capitulating to the ANC's demands during this period. Ramaphosa prefers to describe the ultimate success of the relationship as a result of Meyer's foresight: 'He is a person who saw the light much earlier that many of his colleagues. He acted very cleverly when he realised that changes had to be effected in this country by going all the way, co-operating and not being a stumbling block.' Their success was not based on friendship, as many claimed. Ramaphosa said at the time, *'I think we have a relationship that lends itself to enabling us to resolve problems. I wouldn't say we have become friends. We know that we are adversaries and that we are going to be fighting the elections on different sides … I think we are bound by a common vision of making sure that we move our country from an apartheid society to a democratic one and that is what binds us together.'*

# Shocked back to the negotiating table

**September 1992**

In the meantime, the ANC continued its mass action campaign, which culminated in a march on Bisho, the capital of the 'independent' Ciskei homeland in the Eastern Cape on 7 September 1992. 80 000 people participated in a protest to oust the Ciskei's unpopular military leader, Colonel Oupa Gqozo. But Ciskeian soldiers opened fire on the protesters and 29 people died and over 200 were injured. The media accused ANC leaders of having been 'reckless' in leading the march while also recognising that it was the government's 'surrogates' who were responsible for the deaths of so many people.

While Boipatong had caused the negotiations to be broken off, the bloodshed at Bisho stunned both sides and drove them back to the negotiating table. Behind the scenes, the Cyril-Roelf channel made substantial progress in the face of the violence. The two men concurred that they would first try to reach agreement on a bilateral basis before approaching the other parties for multilateral negotiations.

In a highly dramatic moment De Klerk announced that the government would accept the ANC's demands in relation to the banning of cultural weapons, the fencing off of hostels and the release of political prisoners. For the ANC, De Klerk's announcement represented the 'beginning of the end'. According to Mac Maharaj:

*'This is the point at which De Klerk actually acknowledged that from talking and destabilising he can only move into the future South Africa through some understanding and relationship with the ANC.'*

Valli Moosa believed that, *'The National Party itself was becoming more and more divided, more and more weakened internally, less and less cohesive, the system of alliances which they set up had broken down completely. The popularity of De Klerk had continued to plummet over the past two years and the ANC's popularity had continued to increase.'*

1

# African National Congress

51 Plein Street
Johannesburg 2001
P O Box 61884
Marshalltown 2107

Tel: (011) 330-7000
Fax: (011) 333-9090
Telex: 421252

## OFFICE OF THE PRESIDENT

13 September 1992

Mr F. W. De Klerk
The State President
Pretoria
0001

Per telefax : 012 342 2947 (H)
012 323 8866 (W)

Dear Mr De Klerk

I refer to the public statement you made on 9 September 1992 in the context of the Bisho massacre, and the statement released by the National Working Committee of the ANC on 10 September 1992.

More specifically, the National Working Committee of the ANC noted your call for an urgent meeting between a government delegation led by yourself and an ANC delegation to be led by myself.

In this regard, the National Working Committee of the ANC decided that we are prepared to participate in such a summit. However, it would be a disaster for the country as a whole if it failed to produce concrete results. It is therefore neccessary that the proposed summit be preceded by thorough preparations through the present channels existing between your government and the ANC .

I wish to ensure that there are no misunderstandings between us about the process. The channel between your Mr Roelf Meyer and Mr Cyril Ramaphosa has so far concerned itself with arriving at an understanding about the content of your response to the issues raised in the statement of the National Executive Committee dated 23 June 1992 and in the memoranda exchanged between the government and the ANC. It is crucial to the process that they should complete this task as part of the preparations for the proposed summit.

You are no doubt aware that the issues of the release of the remaining political prisoners and concrete measures to implement the reccomendations of the Goldstone Commission with regard to

**The People Shall Govern!**

---

curbing the violence need to be seen to be carried out. This would include steps to ensure there is a climate of free political activity throughout South Africa, including the so-called self-governing and independent territories.

Unless these issues are resolved satisfactorily, preparations for the proposed summit will be fatally flawed and incomplete.

On this basis, we propose therefore to expand the task of the existing channel to include other aspects which would thoroughly and effectively prepare for the proposed summit.

In conclusion, I wish to draw your attention to pronouncements by leading officers of your army - statements which are calculated to heighten tension, are party political in nature, totally unsubstantiated and extremely harmful to the process of peaceful resolution of the crisis facing our country. I refer in particular to the recent statement by the Chief of the Army, Lieutenant-General Meiring which alleges that Umkhonto We Sizwe has plans underfoot to assassinate Brigadier Gqozo. I need not remind you that it is the same Lt-General Meiring who publically defended Battalion 32 and stated that it would not be disbanded when the Goldstone Commission reccomended this course of action.

Yours sincerely

N.R. MANDELA
PRESIDENT

---

Die Staatspresident
The State President
Pretoria

Mr N R Mandela
President of the African National Congress
P O Box 61884
MARSHALLTOWN
2107

16 September 1992

Dear Mr Mandela

Thank you for your letter received per fax on the morning of 14 September 1992.

It is my conviction that the state of violence in our country and particularly certain recent occurrences resulting in the loss of life, have made it imperative for us to meet urgently to discuss violence related issues; to give new direction and impetus in the search for solutions; and to fulfill our obligation to our people by becoming personally involved in the exchange of ideas. This approach does not provide for the setting of preconditions.

The original reaction from the ANC left the impression with me that you were in broad agreement with this approach. Your letter on Monday, however, seemed to indicate that you would be prepared to meet me only after a number of wide ranging issues have been resolved. This was followed by the publication in Tuesday's Star of an interview in which you revealed a much more flexible approach. The Government publicly welcomed your approach.

In the meantime, ideas on the meeting have been exchanged through Messrs Ramaphosa and Meyer. Bearing in mind the discussions that have already taken place between them, news-paper reports and other communications, I now formally propose that we meet on a date which should be settled within the next 48 hours by Messrs Ramaphosa and Meyer. They can also attend to the practical arrangements such as the agenda, venue and other details.

---

-2-

I agree that proper preparations should be made for the meeting and therefore that delegations led by them, should attempt to complete the record of understanding before the meeting. Should they fail to do so, the outstanding items should be dealt with at the meeting itself. I am confident that agreement can be reached on the record of understanding but cannot agree to make the fact of our meeting dependent on that.

I am looking forward to an early and positive reply.

Yours sincerely

F W DE KLERK

---

# Record of Understanding

**September 1992**

On 26 September 1992, Mandela and De Klerk sealed their new commitment to negotiations by signing the milestone Record of Understanding:

*'Finally, with regard to the constitutional process which was aborted in June this year, common understanding has been reached today in the joint Record of Understanding that we need to move with all urgency towards an interim government of national unity and a democratically elected constituent assembly.*

*It is only the achievement of these goals that will finally bring lasting peace to this blood-soaked land. The points of agreement outlined in the Record of Understanding constitute an important step forward toward breaking the Codesa 2 deadlock. There is obviously still much work to be done to complete this process.'*

In retrospect, both the NP and the ANC saw Bisho as crucial in paving the way towards a final settlement, although each side offered very different views of what had brought about the change.

De Klerk held that *'The period between the break-up of Codesa and Bisho was crucial in the constitutional process. In this period, the ANC was devoted to making the country ungovernable, which they promised when they walked out of Codesa ... They were anxious to save face because they failed – what they threatened did not materialise and so they returned to the negotiating table.'*

For the ANC's Albie Sachs, *'Mass action was the decisive factor in the history of negotiations. It was also very important for morale in the ANC because people were becoming increasingly restive. We re-established for the world to know that the real strength of the country lay with this broad mass of black people living in the townships, organised in unions and civics who wanted change and wouldn't accept some Mickey Mouse kind of a deal.'*

# The right wing stays out

The Record of Understanding dramatically shifted political alliances. The common perception of Codesa 1 was that the ANC and the Patriotic Front had lined up on one side of the table and the government and its allies on the other. After the Record of Understanding, commentators observed that the government and the ANC became the joint driving forces of the process. Everybody else could either become part of that process or stay out of it.

Indeed, both the black and white conservative parties were appalled by this new situation and united in a new bloc. Buthelezi withdrew all contact with the NP, making it clear that he was highly 'insulted' that the government was cutting deals with the ANC without him. He told his supporters at a Shaka Day rally that the agreement was 'an attempt to wipe us off the face of earth as Zulus' and that 'Mr De Klerk has made a fundamental mistake … I am appalled and disgusted and so is the IFP and KwaZulu Government.'

In reaction the IFP, CP, homeland governments and right-wing Afrikaner parties formed the Concerned South Africans Group (Cosag). These strange bedfellows who did not share the same views created an uneasy alliance. But they were united in their determination to scrap the Record of Understanding and stop the ANC and NP uniting against them. They pressed for a federal constitution to preserve the rights of ethnic minorities, especially those of the Zulu and white communities. Talk of secession entered the political arena. Chief Buthelezi and King Goodwill Zwelithini demanded that KwaZulu-Natal be declared an independent, sovereign Zulu state and asked their followers to defend this ideal with their lives if necessary.

Both the NP and ANC recognised that the right wing had the ability to 'create complete chaos' if left out in the cold and that the right wing needed to be 'part of the solution'. Of the alliance between the ANC and the NP at this time, Ramaphosa has said that it was one of the greatest successes of the transition period. 'It is akin to the story of the caravan in the desert which just moves on and on while the dogs are barking.'

**1** A protest against those believed to be responsible for the Bisho Massacre. © *Adil Bradlow*

**2** Poster produced after the Bisho Massacre. © *South African History Archives*

**3** Cosag members Bophuthatswana President Lucas Mangope, Conservative Party leader Ferdi Hartzenberg, leader of the IFP Chief Mangosuthu Buthelezi, and Bophuthatswana delegate Rowan Cronje. © *Avusa*

**1**

FROM THE DESK OF
## NELSON MANDELA
TO:

DATE:

SUBJECT:

Conversation with JS   16·12·92

① moral basis has been eroded
values here be a over again to
but · of our struggle.

② Up to about 6-9 mnths ago they
really became prisoners of visions
which they thought would outshine
ANC

③ Economic situation slowing down
cant deliver to their constituency, business

④ Violence has done us damage. Thought
they could weaken ANC & delay
elections - basically failed in
objective to weaken ANC

⑤ Nats face constitutional dilemma
bring about elections before May
1994

15

FROM THE DESK OF
## NELSON MANDELA
TO:

DATE:

SUBJECT:

all these factors explain their conspiracy.

⑥ They truly believed that M. action
would never succeed

Conclusion unduly pressure to reach
settlement · difficult for them to
delay.

We must all ask ourselves, are we
doing enough to end violence. Political
violence & crime are decimating our
people. There is no greater duty than
to end this carnage.
Those who are tempted to think that
violence can stop violence must be
proved wrong.
not only political  but lout crime

Right wing project themselves as but
representing interest of afrikaner - right
wing helped to spread record

16

FROM THE DESK OF
## NELSON MANDELA
TO:

DATE:

SUBJECT:

absolutely unblemished on
probity culture, language of all
people including afrikaner.
appeal to 2 voters to examine our
record. no political force in our
country that has contributed so
much to race-war as ANC.
External observers have always
expressed surprise that despite history
of such terrible discrimination struggle
here not expressed in race.
answer is ANC

17

# The Furore over the Constitutional Court

One of the final issues to cause major trouble for the negotiators was the question of the structure, composition and jurisdiction of the Constitutional Court. Although the idea of a separate court that would safeguard the constitution had been agreed to early on in the negotiations, it was only at this late stage that the issue was addressed in any detail. The Technical Committee for Constitutional Matters drafted a detailed report that it submitted to the Negotiating Council (NC) meeting on 14 September for consideration.

In a historic decision, the NC resolved that the Constitutional Court would have the power of judicial review. This meant that the court would have the authority to determine the legality of Acts of Parliament and refer any laws that were inconsistent with the constitution to Parliament for revision. Previous legislation disallowed any court of law 'to inquire into or to pronounce upon the validity of an Act of Parliament'. This put an end to the Parliamentary sovereignty that had been in force since 1910, and that had allowed the white-only legislature to enact apartheid laws without interference from the courts.

Two issues remained unresolved: the qualifications of prospective judges and the procedure for their appointment. The former issue was settled relatively easily. The issue of procedure of appointment, however, proved far more explosive than anyone imagined. On 11 November, just days before the final plenary session, the ANC and the NP entered into a bilateral agreement to resolve this issue that had now been debated furiously over the last weeks. Kobie Coetsee, then the Minister of Justice and NP negotiator, alerted Tony Leon to the terms of the agreement for the appointment of judges in a fax.

In his autobiography, Leon sums up this agreement as he recalled it: *'The kernel of the document was that all ten of the Court's judges would be appointed by the President and the Cabinet, with four positions reserved for serving (old order) judges. The Chief Justice would be appointed by the President. In other words, the lynchpin of the new legal order would be open to blatant political manipulation ... and would simply ape the discredited appointment mechanism of the past. However, this court would be entrusted with far greater and more sweeping powers than any other in SA's history.'*

The ANC/NP agreement unleashed a small war at Kempton Park. An outraged Leon warned that the ANC/NP agreement would destroy the independence of the judiciary. The media seized on the issue. Impassioned press statements revealed that the legal profession was divided in its response.

The DP threatened to walk out of the process but then realised that this was an opportunity to take up their argument for a Judicial Service Commission (JSC) once again. The JSC was proposed as a diverse body of government and opposition party politicians, lawyers, academics, etc. The DP felt this kind of body would curtail the extent of political interference in the appointment of judges.

Initially, the ANC would not yield. Just before dinner on the final day of talks, Ramaphosa announced that the ANC had accepted that the JSC would play an important role in the appointment of the judges. Dullah Omar, Chief ANC negotiator on the Judiciary, reportedly said, *'If they (DP) had pushed for making the JSC a crucial selection body, we would have been in a really difficult position.'* Finally the issue of the Constitutional Court was settled.

# Draft after draft

The Technical Committee on Constitutional Matters had submitted the first draft constitution to the Negotiating Council on 26 July. Many more drafts followed. The process of finalising the constitution was very slow as negotiators struggled with the last remaining questions of how decision-making would take place in the proposed GNU and how power-sharing would occur at the executive level. Participants' commitment to negotiation was tested to the limit.

Leon Wessels reflects that what was important at this time was the tools of 'constructive ambiguity' and of 'judicial interpretation'. *'Had these tools not been available, the negotiators would still be at loggerheads today. The most telling example was when the right to life was written into the Interim Constitution. Political parties held diametrically opposed views and no compromise was possible. The solution was – let the courts decide. The process thus moved on. The judges were left to interpret the law.'*

On 28 October, the ANC and the NP reached agreement on a provision for two Deputy Presidents in the GNU, the required percentage to elect a Deputy President and the right to cabinet posts. The NP at last abandoned its claim to a veto over the decisions of the cabinet. For the first two weeks of November 1993, negotiators worked through the night, desperate to ensure that the elections would still take place in April 1994. On 16 November, while workmen were laying out the red carpet for the ceremony to ratify the Interim Constitution the next day, De Klerk and Mandela personally became involved in trying to reach a settlement. On 17 November, Ramaphosa and Meyer hammered out a 'six-pack' agreement that consisted of solutions to the last remaining issues. Meyer jubilantly announced that the NP and ANC 'were in tandem on all remaining constitutional issues'. The agreement included repeal of the legislation that granted independence to the 'homelands'; greater independence for the Constitutional Court; and safeguarded boundaries for the nine regions, which would be able to adopt their own constitutions. Institutionalised power-sharing featured prominently in the agreement, reflecting the hard bargaining that had brought the document into being. Significantly, it created a GNU, with participation secured for all parties with more than 5 per cent of the vote in the elections, and it guaranteed the jobs of existing civil servants for five years.

**1** Final negotiations for the Interim Constitution. © *Hassen Ebrahim / Constitutional Assembly*

**2** Valli Moosa, Dullah Omar, Jacob Zuma and Cyril Ramaphosa during the final stages of negotiations for the Interim Constitution. © *Hassen Ebrahim / Constitutional Assembly*

**3** Dullah Omar and Mac Maharaj. © *Hassen Ebrahim / Constitutional Assembly*

# South Africa's Fourth Constitution

**18 November 1993**

During the final negotiations, smaller parties felt that they had been bypassed and were mere rubber stamps in the process. The ANC and NP tried desperately to persuade them to go along with the deal. Finally, in the early hours of 18 November 1993, the MPNP Plenary adopted the Interim Constitution, which would come into effect on 27 April 1994. Justice Ismail Mohammed congratulated the delegates. *'This is the breaking of the dawn for a nation wrestling with its soul. No force can stop or delay our emancipation from our shameful racist past … This is the last mile of freedom.'* Delegates danced in the corridors in the early hours of the morning. They were very tired but there was a great sense of relief.

Cyril Ramaphosa never doubted that this moment would be reached: *'I knew from the very start that we wouldn't fail. The NP was a formidable enemy. They were armed militarily and in terms of resources. But they were completely bereft and poverty stricken when it came to the will and determination to be free. They didn't have it. We had it. Our people were united and they wanted to be free and that is what gave us strength. Even as our people were dying, even as Chris Hani was assassinated, even as Boipatong happened, we just continued to fix our eyes on that goal.*

*I never, even for a moment, thought we would fail and I knew that our victory was very certain. Nothing could stop this tidal wave towards freedom.'*

The Interim Constitution was passed on 22 November 1993 by the last Parliament under the old order. This was South Africa's fourth constitution but its first democratic one. It set in place a revolutionary principle in South Africa's constitutional history – that the Constitution would be supreme and there would be judicial review to enforce it. For Ramaphosa, it was *'a firm foundation upon which the dreams of millions of South Africans could be realised'.*

For De Klerk, the Constitution 'was not exactly what the NP wanted'. *'We would have liked to have seen something closer to the power – sharing in the Swiss or Belgium model. We would like more clearly defined rights for the regions and minorities. But we were satisfied that we had substantially succeeded in achieving the package that I had spelled out as our bottom line during the referendum the year before.'*

**4** Joe Slovo and Roelf Meyer greeting each other at the opening of the TEC, November 1993.
© *Adil Bradlow / Oryx Archives*

**5** Cyril Ramaphosa and Colin Eglin at the opening of the TEC, November 1993.
© *Adil Bradlow / Oryx Archives*

**6** Roelf Meyer presenting Cyril Ramaphosa with a cake to celebrate his birthday, which is on the same day the Interim Constitution was adopted.
© *Hassen Ebrahim / Constitutional Assembly*

**4**

**5**

**6**

# National unity and reconciliation

The most celebrated features of the Interim Constitution were its Bill of Rights and its explicit commitment to reconciliation and national unity. The Interim Constitution famously states:

*'This Constitution provides a historic bridge between the past of a deeply divided society characterised by strife, conflict, untold suffering and injustice, and a future founded on the recognition of human rights, democracy and peaceful co-existence and development opportunities for all South Africans, irrespective of colour, race, class, belief or sex.*

*'The pursuit of national unity, the wellbeing of all South African citizens and peace require reconciliation between the people of South Africa and the reconstruction of society.*

*'The adoption of this Constitution lays the secure foundation for the people of South Africa to transcend the divisions and strife of the past, which generated gross violations of human rights, the transgression of humanitarian principles in violent conflicts and a legacy of hatred, fear, guilt and revenge.*

*'These can now be addressed on the basis that there is a need for understanding but not for vengeance, a need for reparation but not for retaliation, a need for ubuntu but not for victimisation.*

*'In order to advance such reconciliation and reconstruction, amnesty shall be granted in respect of acts, omissions and offences associated with political objectives and committed in the course of the conflicts of the past. To this end, Parliament under this Constitution shall adopt a law determining a firm cut-off date, which shall be a date after 8 October 1990 and before 6 December 1993,*

*and providing for the mechanisms, criteria and procedures, including tribunals, if any, through which such amnesty shall be dealt with at any time after the law has been passed.'*

The Constitution ends with the following words:

*'With this Constitution and these commitments we, the people of South Africa, open a new chapter in the history of our country.*

*'Nkosi sikelel' iAfrika.*
*God seën Suid-Afrika.*
*Morena boloka sechaba sa heso.*
*May God bless our country.*
*Mudzimu fhatutshedza Afrika.*
*Hosi katekisa Afrika.'*

When this epilogue was finally adopted, Leon Wessels noted, *'Many of us gave a sigh of relief for the fact that we could have the full truth out in the open without vengeance … those ringing words that provided for a process of uncovering the whole truth and the granting of amnesty marked the beginning of the long road of reconciliation.'*

1

# The first democratic elections

27 April
1994

On 27 April 1994, South Africans of all races went to the polls for the first time in the country's history. Prophets of doom expected bloodshed and civil strife on the day. Instead, South Africa rose to the challenge. Peace prevailed and the elections took place in an atmosphere of complete calm. An old miner, who stood among 10 000 miners in the longest queue imaginable, stopped Cyril Ramaphosa on his way to vote. His simple words sum up the heart-felt jubilation of the day: *'What we fought for all these years has now been attained. I can now go and retire and die.'*

Nelson Mandela's announcement of the ANC election victory in Johannesburg struck a perfect note of celebration of his party's success while still emphasising reconciliation amongst all.

*'This is one of the most important moments in the life of our country. I stand here before you filled with deep pride and joy - pride in the ordinary, humble people of this country. You have shown such a calm, patient determination to reclaim this country as your own, and joy that we can loudly proclaim from the rooftops "free at last!" ...*

*Tomorrow, the entire ANC leadership and I will be back at our desks. We are rolling up our sleeves to begin tackling the problems our country faces. We ask you all to join us, go back to your jobs in the morning. Let's get South Africa working.*

*For we must, together and without delay, begin to build a better life for all South Africans. ...*

*I hold out a hand of friendship to the leaders of all parties and their members, and ask all of them to join us in working together to tackle the problems we face as a nation. An ANC government will serve all the people of South Africa, not just ANC members ... Now is the time for celebration, for South Africans to join together to celebrate the birth of democracy. I raise a glass to you all for working so hard to achieve what can only be called a small miracle ... Let us build the future together, and toast a better life for all South Africans.'*

1 The ballot paper for the first democratic elections. The IFP sticker had to be pasted onto the bottom at the last minute. © *Independent Electoral Commission*

2 Voters queuing in the first democratic elections, 27 April 1994. © *Graeme Williams*

1

**1** Many voters had to queue for hours to cast their votes. © *Benny Gool / Oryx Archives*

# The inauguration

**10 May 1994**

Just after noon at the Union Buildings in Pretoria, Nelson Rolihlahla Mandela, the first President of the new, democratic South Africa took the Oath of Office. The vast crowds who had gathered on the lawns of the amphitheatre cheered wildly as Mandela, standing between his two Deputy Presidents, Thabo Mbeki and FW de Klerk, lifted their arms into the air in a sign of victory. Military jets flew overhead in perfect formation. Mandela stepped on to a special bullet-proof stage and proclaimed to the fledgling nation:

*'The time for healing the wounds has come. The moment to bridge the chasm that divides us has come ... We have triumphed in our effort to implant hope in the breasts of the millions of our people. We enter into a covenant that we shall build a society in which all South Africans, both black and white, will be able to walk tall ... a rainbow nation at peace with itself and the world.'*

In his address to the people of Cape Town on his election as President the previous day, he said:

*'We place our vision of a new constitutional order for South Africa on the table not as conquerors, prescribing to the conquered. We speak as fellow citizens to heal the wounds of the past with the intent of constructing a new order based on justice for all. This is the challenge that faces all South Africans today, and it is one to which I am certain we will all rise.'*

**1** Nelson Mandela taking the Oath of Office during his inauguration as President at the Union Buildings. © *Avusa*

**2** Crowds gathered on the lawns in front of the Union Buildings in celebration of the inauguration of Nelson Mandela. © *Avusa*

# The South African miracle

10 May
1994

Across the globe, South Africa was heralded as the 'miracle nation'. For the majority of South Africans, the so-called miracle was the long-awaited outcome of decades of struggle and much heartache. For the political parties involved, it had taken much courage and persistence to overcome the tremendous obstacles stacked up against them.

Looking back on this period, most commentators differ in defining the 'magical' ingredients of this negotiated transition. Some believe that the success of process was due to the fact that it was fluid and unpredictable and it was not based on any international model or the edicts of any particular party. Common wisdom holds that if either side had tried to say in advance how it was going to work, both sides would have rejected it. Valli Moosa agreed: *'If one looks back now I don't think anybody had a completely coherent blueprint of the transition process. Everybody had a vision, different parties had their bottom lines, but it was virtually impossible to have a coherent blueprint. It is something that emerged over a period of time.'*

Other commentators have emphasised the personalities of the negotiators and the chemistry that developed in particular between Cyril and Roelf. For others, this aspect of the process has been exaggerated. Though the 'Roelf and Cyril' relationship was crucial, they believe that the many bilateral and multilateral channels established to make decisions on specific issues also aided the process enormously.

Whatever the interpretation, the one incontrovertible truth is that former antagonists had sat around the same table and hammered out a settlement for a new South Africa. In the process, all sides learnt to compromise, make concessions, justify their positions and move away from unhelpful solutions. Negotiators were now far better prepared to take on the task of writing the final Constitution.

Most importantly, all the main roleplayers concurred that despite the tumultuous moments and hardships, the country was still functioning. In Dawie de Villiers, opinion: *'The remarkable thing is that we had a peaceful transition. Things go on as in the past. The farmers are farming, businesses are doing business, people are travelling … We lose sight of the reality of how hot that room was and what we have achieved.'*

Valli Moosa summed up the situation at the end of the process:

*'The Interim Constitution is an instrument for the transformation of this country. It could well have been called the Transition to Democracy Act. It's long, it's convoluted and has all kinds of details that other constitutions in the world do not have. It serves the ideals that the nation now stands for. While the white community may not necessarily like the ANC … there isn't a general sort of move amongst whites that they should attempt to return to the old ways of apartheid.'*

1 President Mandela raises the hand of his Deputy, FW de Klerk, in celebration of the first democratic government. © *The Bigger Picture / Reuters*

# The Countdown of One Law for One Nation

## 1994-1995

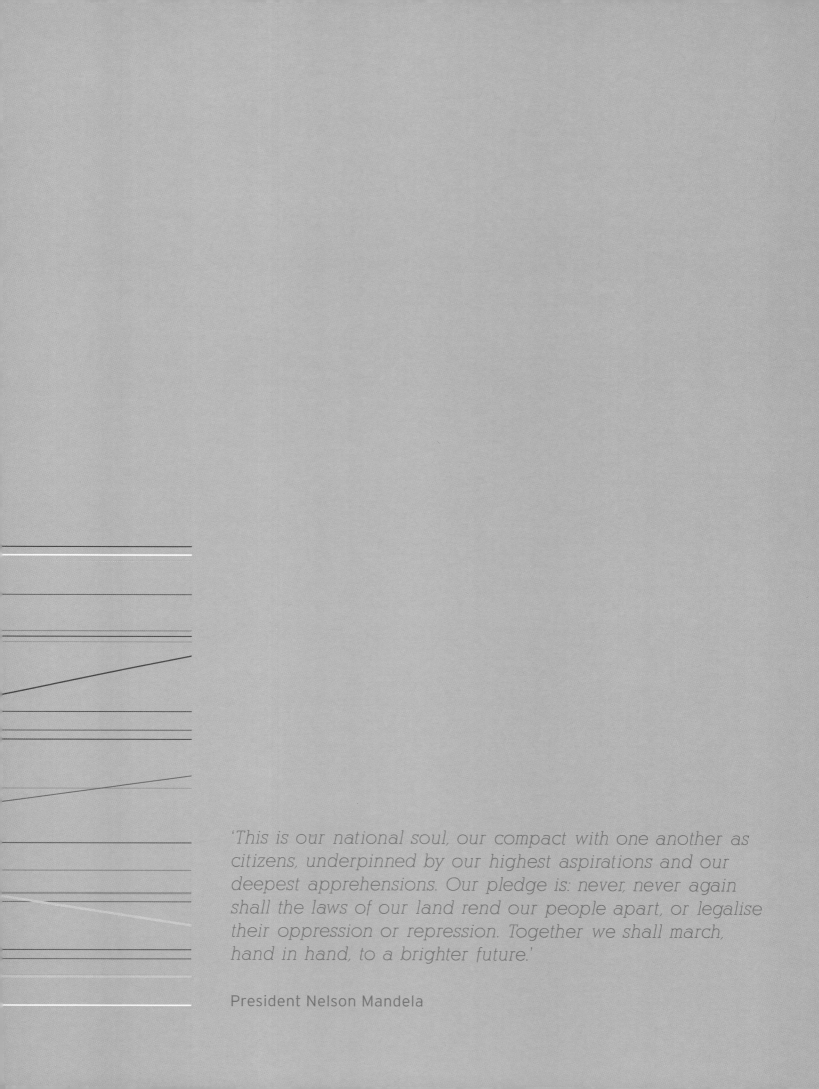

'This is our national soul, our compact with one another as citizens, underpinned by our highest aspirations and our deepest apprehensions. Our pledge is: never, never again shall the laws of our land rend our people apart, or legalise their oppression or repression. Together we shall march, hand in hand, to a brighter future.'

President Nelson Mandela

1

At the first Constitutional Assembly meeting in August 1994, key participants expressed the importance of the task that lay ahead:

*'We are embarking on what is perhaps the most important task that any of us will ever be called upon to do ... to decide on the rules and the structures by which South Africa will be governed. This Constitutional Assembly's decisions will have a profound impact, not only on the process of government ... but on the quality of many people's lives and on the extent of the freedom that our people are going to enjoy.'* - Colin Eglin, Democratic Party

*'The meeting of this Assembly today is a manifestation of what was a dream for years, a dream which finally came true at the polls in April. It is on the basis of the new constitution that we will systematically effect fundamental long-term changes. It will be the supreme law to ensure that the ills that have plagued our society do not become the lot of generations to come.'* - Baleka Mbete-Kgositsile, ANC MP

*'South Africa is the envy of the world and the constitution-making process is causing international excitement. We have had the elections and the political baggage is largely out of the way. Now we have the luxury of revisiting and sharpening up our constitutional ideas to create a new and modern document that will serve South Africa for generations to come.'* - Leon Wessels, National Party

Others laid out the challenges, aspirations and complexities that they felt at the outset of the process:

*'The constitution we write for South Africa will only succeed if it is the product of what is in the hearts and the minds of all South Africans, not only the majority. The problem of satisfying the Afrikaner's desire for self-determination is a very complex matter.'* - Dr Corné Mulder, Freedom Front MP

*'We are not talking about something that is fixed, but about a bubble that may burst. It is very wise for us to approach debate in the Constitutional Assembly knowing that we have something which might be more fragile than we think and that we must work towards the strengthening of the whole process.'* - Walter Felgate, IFP MP

*'A genuinely South African constitution should redefine our society and rewrite the history of our country so as to demonstrate and reflect that South Africa is not a European country which happens to be in Africa, but is an African country.'* - RK Sizani, PAC MP

*'The ACDP believes the future of our country will be best secured by a form of government which we should like to refer to as a "constitutional republic" with an entrenched Bill of Rights based on biblical principles. We need to define what the word of God has to say concerning a framework for a godly government.'* - LM Green, ACDP MP

*'The ACDP would like to see a constitution that is the supreme law of the land, a constitution that protects not only the rights of individuals but also those of unborn children. The ACDP wishes to see a constitution that will be legitimate, enduring and that upholds biblical, family and traditional values.'* - Rev. KR Meshoe, Leader of the ACDP

# A seemingly distant deadline

## August 1994

21 months to deadline

The initial spirit of optimism amongst drafters in meeting all of the challenges was understandable. The task that lay ahead was no longer to create the kind of 'peace treaty' containing 'grand compromises' on all sides, as Kader Asmal described the Interim Constitution, but was rather about people getting a job done within set parameters and time frames. The political landscape outside of the negotiating chamber was also far less volatile. As Leon Wessels remarked, *'At Kempton Park ... we had to focus on breaking the political deadlock that had polarised the country. We had to deal with the question of the transition from one order to another. That was essentially a political settlement we were crafting. Here, we will not be dealing with transitional matters. We are dealing with a constitution that will stand the test of time and take us into the twenty-first century.'*

Importantly, the Constitutional Assembly was also able to create the administrative machinery necessary for the drafting of the constitution with the advantage of hindsight of the Codesa experience. Hassen Ebrahim, who had been intimately involved throughout Kempton Park, was appointed the executive director of the administration and Marion Sparg and Louisa Zondo his two deputies. They felt mixed emotions at the outset.

*'We were overwhelmed and frightened by the nature of the assignment. There had never been a process like this anywhere ... With my two deputies, we hired a very diverse staff that came from the liberation movements, political party offices, the civil service. But they all had one thing in common – they were prepared to work for long and unpredictable hours and give up two years of their lives for a common cause.'*

In the end, about 120 people were contracted to provide technical, legal, research and financial back-up to the negotiators. Receptionists, accountants, travel clerks, media liaison officers, campaign managers and writers worked day and night for two years in a four-floor office space in Adderley Street, Cape Town, to perform the varied tasks required by the constitution-writing process. These ranged from setting up banquet dinners for a thousand VIPs to writing copy for advertisements and drafting legislation. By the end of the process, over 20 million photocopies had been made and almost as many cups of coffee had been drunk.

1

**1** Leon Wessels inside the Parliament building. © *Subash Jeram / Constitutional Assembly*

**2** Tony Leon from the DP during a debate in the Constitutional Assembly. © *Subash Jeram / Constitutional Assembly*

**3** Business sector hearing in the Constitutional Assembly. © *Subash Jeram / Constitutional Assembly*

# The Constitutional Committee

A Constitutional Committee was established as the engine room of the process. It consisted of 44 members nominated by parties in proportion to their representation, although some smaller parties were granted full representation. The committee's manageable size made quick decision-making easier. This structure ultimately allowed the tight deadlines to be met. An independent panel of constitutional experts was set up to resolve conflicts, avoid deadlocks between parties and give advice on technical issues.

The committee met in the old House of Assembly Chamber of Parliament. This room, with its heavy wood panelling and green leather seating, had been the citadel of white power for 90 years. 'It was the bull-ring, the cockpit of all the political struggles,' explained Colin Eglin, an opposition MP under the old order for 30 years. *It was the very room in which Dr Verwoerd was assassinated; the room in which the old United Party split and Hertzog and Smuts parted ways on the war issue; the room Malan walked into in May 1948 as the new National Party Prime Minister of South Africa. It is where Vorster, Botha and then later De Klerk governed from.* It was now to become the space where all the important decisions regarding the new constitution would be taken.

Leon Wessels admitted that the NP carried the burden of their history in this chamber and were more challenged that the other parties to some extent:

*'The NP had to transform itself and make a claim on issues which were not part of their armory in the decades that preceded that. The NP is still coming to grips with its own past and, in doing so, projecting itself into the future. The ANC and DP had more of a history with some of the issues of federalism and individual rights.'*

Piet Marais added that the NP also had to get used to a completely new *modus operandi*:

*'In the past, the debates tended to be worthless because the majority party made the decision somewhere in Cabinet. Even we as ordinary members of Parliament were not much more than rubber stamps. We listened in our caucus to what Cabinet decided and then we came in here and we supported that. Now the whole situation is much more transparent and there's a lot more participation, also from the public at large.'*

2

3

# Constitutional Talk – No. 9 SHAPING THE FUTURE

*It is in the 46-person Constitutional Committee that seasoned negotiators and new Parliamentarians get down to the nitty-gritty of drafting the document that will be the supreme law of the land. And, word by word, phrase by phrase, as it is read and discussed, our new constitution is taking shape.*

The driving winter rain drums against the windows of the historic Good Hope chamber in the Parliamentary complex, but the men and women inside pay no heed. Instead, they bend their eyes and minds to the draft clauses before them and debate the content, spirit and likely consequences of practically every word.

Chairing the proceedings are not one but two people, squeezed together in the Chairperson's bench. Cyril Ramaphosa and Leon Wessels, Chairperson and Deputy of the Constitutional Assembly, are a combination unthinkable just a few years ago. But now these veterans of many, many hours of negotiations are procedural allies as well as political adversaries.

Each of the six political parties has representation on the Constitutional Committee in proportion to their support in Parliament. Yet the smaller parties contribute their fair share to the debate, spelling out their positions, suggesting alternative drafts and finding themselves in harmony with parties at opposing ends of the political spectrum at times.

Ramaphosa, alternating with Wessels, guides the debate, gently chiding the members when they react with exasperation to familiar rhetoric.

*'This is a democratic process. Everyone shall be heard,'* he says.

It is not all deadly serious. A member raises laughter when he quotes the old saying that there is no such thing as freedom 'until the children are married and the dog has died'. There is also light relief in the teasing exchanges between political foes who know each other and their idiosyncrasies well.

But for the rest it is hard work. The technical experts, constitutional lawyers and academics explain phrases that are not clear, quoting from constitutions in newly reconstructed Eastern European countries, Latin America and Africa as well as the better-known ones like the Canadian and the American.

The long day is punctuated by breaks for tea and plates of rather ordinary biscuits. At mid-day committee members brave the freezing wind and driving rain to get something to eat.

As the afternoon darkens into evening and the wrought-iron chandeliers blaze ever more brightly, patience wears thin and other commitments – families and Parliamentary obligations – beckon. A few clauses have been accepted, many have been sent back to the technical advisors for redrafting.

For the weary members, it may have been just another day at the office but is one full of historic significance. It is another step on a truly exceptional journey, one that few people witness or participate in in their lifetimes.

Only the Inkatha Freedom Party is absent; the party has withdrawn from the CA structures over the question of international mediation.

For the others, the agendas are clear and, while there is much consensus, some issues will always stir heated debate at each step of the process.

# South Africa's New Constitution is being written.

Make sure it contains your ideas – it is your democracy!!
Below is a guide for sending in your ideas.

Write down your ideas and fold this form on the dotted lines.
Post it as soon as possible

**Your Name:**

**Your Address:** Mfinizo A/A

**Contact Telephone Number:**

## Ideas/proposals/submissions

### A. What my problems / issues / concerns are ...

1. Inkosi Asiyifuni kuba Abantu Ayibenzekinto
2. Ndifuna Sakhelwe imizi Mveliso yokusebe nza kuba Sidinga imisebenzi.
3. Masanbiselwe Amaziko ezempilo.
4. Masifumane imfundo yamahala.
5. Masoncezelwe izikolo zethu.
6. Masifakelwe Amanzi nombane.
7. Umntu ozelwe ekhubazekile maahole inkamnkam ubom bakhe bonke.

### B. What I think the new constitution should say about this ...

1. Mayivulwe intsango isetenziswe ngoku semthethweni kuba intanga Abantu Abagulayo zizifuba.
2. Umntu obulele omnye umntu makafume ne isohlwayo seminyaka engashumi amahlanu esonisanzima.
3. Amapolisa makapyeke ukungena erindlini ze makasebenze erindleleni kuphela.

THE NEW CONSTITUTION

347

# From Paarl to Peddie

**February 1995**

16 months to deadline

The Constitutional Assembly also convened face-to-face meetings across the country that were dubbed by the press 'the constitutional road-show'. This process targeted rural and disadvantaged communities who were often marginalised from the mainstream political processes and were unlikely to access information through print or electronic media. This was the only time in South Africa's history that official politicians had gone to the people without canvassing for votes or seeking party political support. The process most closely resembled the Freedom Charter campaign in the 1950s, when volunteers had gone from door to door to collect people's demands.

The meetings began in Paarl, near Cape Town, where Ramaphosa addressed about 600 residents. Over the next few months, residents of informal settlements and big and small towns across the country were all afforded the opportunity to make oral submissions on issues pertaining to the writing of the new constitution. *Constitutional Talk* newspaper declared:

'From Paarl to Peddie, from Ellisras in the north to Saldanha in the west, members of the Constitutional Assembly have crisscrossed South Africa to hear the views of the people. At the 22 Constitutional Public Meetings, crowds have ranged from 130 to over 4 000 and the response generally has been enthusiastic.'

While describing Ramaphosa as a forceful, sharp and diligent chairperson inside Parliament, Leon Wessels has remarked that he was at his very best when he had the opportunity to interact with the public at these meetings: *'Before a visit to the Western Cape town of Paarl I said: "Cyril, this is Afrikaans country. You cannot hope to win the people over if you speak English." Ramaphosa addressed the rather conservative Paarl community in Afrikaans that day. He relished displaying his multilingualism – and he had the crowd eating out of his hand.'*

In truth, when it came to enthusiasm for the Public Participation Programme, it was hard to match that of Leon Wessels himself. In his role as Deputy Chairperson, a new world had opened up for him. He later commented that his involvement in the Constitutional Assembly 'represented the pinnacle of my personal political career'. At the time he enthused:

'It is a wonderful process to be involved in ... It is all typically South African with the smooth edges as well as the rough ones, the many different views and beliefs, all the excitement and frustration. There are deep differences, but with a common loyalty to this country and a will to find each other, we can overcome them. And I am proud to be part of it.'

In the end, more than a thousand workshops reached approximately 95 000 members of the public. So-called national sector hearings were held in Pretoria, Johannesburg and Cape Town, dealing with business, children's rights, traditional leaders, religious groups, youth, labour and women. The *Constitutional Assembly Annual Report* stated:

'By empowering civil society to participate in the constitution-making process, the Constitutional Assembly was able to add a new dimension to the development of democracy in South Africa. This was the key component of the strategy to make the constitution-making process a people-driven process.'

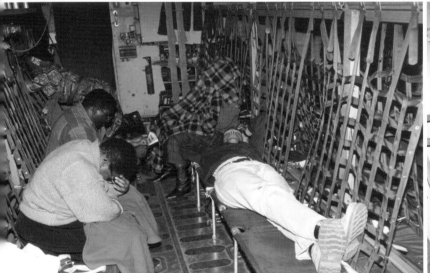

**1** Members of the Constitutional Assembly travelling on a military Dakota to one of the public meetings. © *Subash Jeram / Constitutional Assembly*

# The nation's issues

The kinds of issues raised in the submissions varied considerably, ranging from animal rights to gun ownership, from pornography to abortion and Afrikaans as an official language. The bulk related to human rights issues, particularly the 'right to life' and 'second-generation rights' like the right to education, housing and jobs. Most contentious during this process were objections to the sexual orientation clause and to the secular nature of the state.

But the most humbling, according to Paul Davids, were *'the ones from ordinary people who just want the basic things in life. Sometimes they don't even have a proper piece of paper to write on and they can hardly express themselves, but they send in their deepest thoughts. Some of them bring tears to the eyes. It is so easy to take people for granted, but this process has reminded me there is more to each person than meets the eye.'*

**1-5** Members of the public passionately make their view heard at one of the many public meetings held around the country. © *Subash Jeram / Constitutional Assembly*

# Behind the scenes

## March 1995

15 months to deadline

While vast numbers of South Africans communicated their opinions in the many different forums that had been created, the negotiators continued their work behind the scenes. They had agreed to produce the first working draft of the constitution according to a strict timetable set out in the work plan, referred to by the administrators as 'the heart of the process'. According to this plan, the first draft of the constitution would be completed by August 1995. Hurdles were starting to emerge. The time frame was one of the major issues. As the NP's Sheila Camerer said, *'There's a great deal of cheerfulness around, but the trouble is that we're operating against a deadline and I don't think there's a hope in Hades of getting there if we carry on with the process as it is. We have piles of reports, but there hasn't been a single agreement that has been finalised.'*

A serious setback occurred in March 1995 when the IFP members walked out of Parliament. Buthelezi was angered and insulted by what he pronounced as the 'government's failure to honour their agreement around international mediation'. The IFP still hoped to gain greater provincial autonomy through a mediation process. Buthelezi accused the ANC of running the country through majoritarianism rather than consensus and said that the IFP would not take part in the Constitutional Assembly. He also declared that his party would not accept the constitution.

The IFP's departure altered the balance of power in the Assembly. The new constitution had to be passed by 327 votes and the ANC was just 15 votes short of this. The NP became a critical negotiating partner. The ANC's Valli Moosa explained: *'Without the NP, it was unlikely that the constitution would be adopted, because if the NP did not vote in favour of the Constitution, chances were that all the other smaller opposition parties would then also vote against the Constitution.'*

Ramaphosa and others insisted that the IFP walkout would not delay the process. 'The IFP lost a golden, historic opportunity to drive home their demands to the ANC and only history will judge them,' reflected Ramaphosa at the end of the process.

1 Special-edition poster for the Constitutional Assembly. © *Constitutional Assembly*

2 Zapiro cartoon, date, 12 April 1995. © *Zapiro*

# May 1995

## 13 months to deadline

Many people and organisations were making their voices heard on the streets of South Africa at this time, marching to Parliament to present their petitions to the Constitutional Assembly. The ACDP and the Christian Voice organised a protest march in a campaign to give the constitution an overtly Christian character. Bearing placards decrying a godless state, thousands of fervent Christians shouted, 'Don't forget Jesus,' as they delivered their memorandum. Without God's authority, Ramaphosa was told, the Constitution would not have any legitimacy. Church leaders said they feared that the government was prejudiced against Christianity because of the bias towards the religion during the apartheid era. They criticised the 'flood of pornography' entering the country, the repeal of censorship laws and the possibility of abortion on demand being legalised.

Holding a Bible in his hand, Ramaphosa responded that he was a Christian himself, as were many of the elected representatives then drafting the Constitution. He denied there was any move to ban religion or 'do away with God', saying the Constitution being drafted went further than many others in protecting freedom of religious belief and the right to worship. However, in a democracy these rights had to be afforded equally to other religions such as the Islamic and Jewish faiths. He assured the marchers that the Constitutional Assembly would pay serious attention to their concerns.

The Equality Foundation, a national coalition of gay and lesbian organisations, also reacted strongly to a attack from the ACDP. A spokesperson, Kevan Botha, argued:

'The constitution promises to discard the past of exclusion and irrational prejudice and to build a future based on freedom and equality for all ... nobody was excluded from that vision. The rich, the poor, men and women, black and white, people of differing social and ethnic backgrounds, the young and the old, heterosexuals, gays and lesbians – we all joined hands in solemnly promising to rid ourselves of intolerance, hatred and disrespect for each other. It would be a travesty if apartheid in any form resurfaced in the formative years of the new South Africa.'

There was much vociferous debate in the media about these contentious issues.

1 Christian protesters marching to Parliament to object to South Africa being declared a secular state. © Constitutional Assembly

# August 1995

## 10 months to deadline

While marches and protests took place outside, the theme committees continued to thrash out several contentious issues behind closed doors. As time went on, it became apparent that the parties were quite far apart on many matters. The upbeat spirit and co-operative alliances that had characterised the first year of the Constitutional Assembly were starting to show signs of dissipating.

By the end of August 1995, it became clear that the first draft constitution would not be tabled as initially planned. Ebrahim appealed for more time. This was reluctantly agreed to, although all political parties still insisted on 10 May 1996 as the final deadline. There were just ten months to go and a draft of the constitution had yet to be produced.

A new subcommittee, known as 'the Bird', was established in a bid to break the deadlocks that had developed. With its supposed 'bird's-eye view' of the process, it was hoped that this initiative would hurry things along. This committee was, however, only partially successful. Ramaphosa conceded that it was 'only bilateral meetings between the parties that can now enhance the process'.

FW de Klerk expressed his own worries about an important issue for the NP – the protection of minority rights. He asserted that his party's demands were 'not a smokescreen to continue to preserve privilege or to maintain a form of separatism or apartheid' but insisted that 'this is what this country needs'.

*'We believe that South Africa with its complex society ... requires formulae which can create win–win situations, which can effectively protect minorities however you define them, whether they are religious, political or cultural minorities ...*

*Only if all the component parts of the total society feel that they are not threatened by being part of this bigger nation, that they won't be trampled upon, that they are not asked to stop being what they are by becoming and being loyal South Africans, will we get the right atmosphere which will make nation building really succeed.'*

1

**1** Constitutional Assembly members debating in the old chamber of Parliament. © *Subash Jeram / Constitutional Assembly*

# The first Working Draft

Finally, in October 1995 the first milestone was reached. The Constitutional Assembly was presented with a completed Refined Working Draft of the constitution. After a year of meeting to discuss submissions and public opinion, there was something real on the table on which to negotiate. The Constitutional Assembly chairperson declared:

*'For the first time since we started we have before us a composite draft constitution that is near completion. We are getting close to finalising the work that we were given to do.'*

These proved to be valiant words. While the text certainly provided the first sense of what the final constitution might look like, it also revealed major issues of contention. For one thing, several politicians were uncomfortable with the 'plain language' approach that had been adopted and many felt that the actual wording failed to reflect the agreements that had been reached. More seriously, technical advisors listed more than 30 issues where agreement was required in principle and a further 130 where negotiation was still needed to refine the clauses. The issues ranged from the influence of minority parties in the executive arm of government to the right to receive education in single-language schools. The politicians let their feelings of discontent with the first draft be known.

*'This is a non-document,'* said the NP's André Fourie. *'We disagree fundamentally [about the need for a property clause in the Bill of Rights],'* declared Sheila Camerer. *'The document fails to reflect some of the agreements or changes that have taken place in bilateral meetings,'* complained Colin Eglin of the DP. *'A Western liberal constitutional order'* is how Richard Sizani of the PAC described the draft.

# The first Working Draft goes public

## November 1995

### 7 months to deadline

Despite political and technical objections to the Working Draft, the Constitutional Assembly approved it in November 1995. On 22 November, over five million copies of the Working Draft in all eleven official languages were printed and distributed throughout the whole country.

The Working Draft once again allowed people to become actively involved in the constitution-making process. A second round of written submissions began pouring in. Yet again, this was a resounding success. From November 1995 to 20 February 1996, the Working Draft Constitution attracted about 250 000 petitions and 1 438 submissions. These were more easily summarised and directly linked to specific articles in the constitution, compared with the first phase. While the public was perusing the draft, Ramaphosa attempted to use the document to woo Mangosuthu Buthelezi back into the Constitutional Assembly.

*'I will be seeking to invite the IFP to come back to the process. When they read this constitution I am sure that they will see that this is the type of constitution that is good for the country.'*

Buthelezi and Ramaphosa never met and the IFP remained outside the process. But negotiations between the other political parties on the shape of the final text picked up pace after the production of the Working Draft. This edition provided parties with the first comprehensive list of outstanding issues to be resolved. The various further editions of the Working Draft formed the basis of further discussions in the 'Bird' sub-committee.

Imithethosisekelo, Umbuso Wentando Yeningi

**KANYE NOHLAKA OLUFINGQIWE**

Lomthethosisekelo Omusha

*The Constitutional Assembly*

**1** Cyril Ramaphosa and Leon Wessels proudly displaying the draft copy of the constitution. © *Subash Jeram / Constitutional Assembly*

**2** Copy of the first draft in Zulu and further refined Working Draft of the constitution. © *Subash Jeram / Constitutional Assembly*

**3** Poster from the Constitutional Assembly media campaign. © *Constitution Assembly*

# The final stage

The Constitutional Assembly

**Y**ou've made
your **mark.**

You've had *your say.*

Now we're making
sure **it counts.**

Right now we, the members of the Constitutional Assembly, are analyzing and discussing the nearly two million submissions and petitions that you, the citizens of our country, have been sending to us since the beginning of the year.

We're making sure that your views are considered as we are at the crucial stage of negotiating our country's new Constitution. We plan to publish draft constitutional text in October this year to give you another opportunity to have your say before the new Constitution is finalised.

*i*t's your *right* to decide your *Constitutional* rights.  THE *NEW* CONSTITUTION

3

*'When you retreat into the bilateral, that's where you really begin to remove the frills, remove the playing to the gallery and actually begin to look each other in the eye and say, "Okay, what is your story?"'*

The administrative staff was feeling more anxious. They had to process the public's submissions and also allow time for the technical drafting of the clauses and for producing the document in plain language. They facilitated many bilateral and multilateral meetings between the parties. Ebrahim concurred with Roelf Meyer's view: 'Although meetings behind closed doors did not augur well with members of the civil society or the media, they allowed for very frank discussions.' Negotiators held on to their optimism.

In mid-March 1996, the Management Committee evaluated progress after considering the fourth edition of the Working Draft. Roelf Meyer observed that 'the more difficult issues had been fairly easily resolved while some of the issues that were originally thought to be of lesser importance became the final stumbling blocks'. These were:

the death penalty: what form should the 'right to life' clause take?
the property clause: to what extent should property have constitutional protection?
the lock-out: should employers be entitled to enforce lock-outs during strikes?
language: what would be the official language?
education: should single-medium schools be allowed?
socio-economic legislation: should the Bill of Rights include these second-tier rights?

The pace of negotiations picked up as the deadline of 8 May approached. Besides the deadlocked issues, a further 54 issues still needed political attention and 25 technical issues needed to be resolved. There was now a serious concern that the final constitution would not be completed by May. The negotiators accepted a proposal mooted by the administration that a multilateral should take place in relative isolation over several days to resolve all outstanding issues. All parties agreed: they were keen to meet the deadline and have a final constitution adopted.

By the beginning of February, as work resumed after the December break, the full magnitude of the task that lay ahead became all too clear. A mild panic began to set in. There were just three months to go and many outstanding issues still had to be resolved. On 15 February 1996, the Management Committee formally recognised 68 issues. Arguments were becoming increasingly heated.

The politicians were still confident that they would make the deadline. Roelf Meyer described the climate as 'conducive to compromise and negotiating' but hinted that there might be some pressure on the process as the politicians 'needed to negotiate behind closed doors so we can allow them to change their minds and positions gracefully'. Baleka Mabete-Kgositsile agreed:

# The Arniston *bosberaad*

## 1–3 April 1996

38 days to
deadline

Between 1 and 3 April 1996, members of political parties, together with their advisors, technical advisors to the Assembly and the Independent Panel of Constitutional Experts, decamped from Parliament to Arniston, a small, secluded seaside village in the Western Cape. The press was kept out of the closed-door sessions held at Die Herberg, a former missile testing station. For the first time in the two-year process, privacy was the order of the day. Reports were later gleaned from participants that the atmosphere was no longer as convivial as it had once been. Ramaphosa tried to inject a jovial spirit when he opened the proceedings. *'This looks like the United Nations,'* he said. *'You all look so serious. There are people here wearing jacket and ties. I'm making a ruling that there are to be no ties and jackets.'*

Tapes of the debates stacked up as politicians waded through the outstanding issues day and night. The progress recorded at this multilateral was significant. A more positive chairperson stated at the end of the proceedings: *'It defies logic; all parties are really happy with their scores. It's a win-win situation for everyone.'*

Roelf Meyer concurred: *'The outstanding items have been reduced to only a few.'*

Negotiators thought that they could now see light at the end of the long negotiating tunnel. They clearly did not anticipate how the four 'outstanding items' that were still unresolved – education, property, the right to life and the lock-out – could potentially jeopardise the entire process. Looking back, Roelf Meyer explains how this situation came about:

*'From the beginning, the ANC and the NP were of the impression that the real stumbling block would be the division of power between the Central Government and the provinces. Often, this issue was referred to as "the heart of the Constitution". We were afraid that we would deadlock on that. At Arniston, we mainly resolved that issue. And then of course other issues that had not been very high up in the mind suddenly came to the fore, like the property clause, education and so forth.'*

A report was tabled at the Constitutional Committee on 4 April. This Committee instructed the Technical Team to produce the fifth and penultimate version of the Working Draft. While they incorporated the new decisions from Arniston, it was time for the negotiators to take an Easter holiday and catch their breath before the final weeks of negotiation began.

1

2

# 'The Channel'

On 15 April 1996, the Constitutional Committee received a copy of the new draft. The committee now had four days to resolve the deadlocked issues and produce a bill to go before the Constitutional Assembly. At this point the 'channel bilateral', a 'two-by-two', was reinstated between Cyril Ramaphosa and Valli Moosa of the ANC and Roelf Meyer and Leon Wessels of the NP. As with the end of the MPNP, the most difficult and retractable issues were referred to that channel. Said Valli Moosa, '"The Channel" again was the strength of the process because we all knew that whenever it came to the push, they were there to take over.' Roelf Meyer commented: 'We were able to use the approach that we had always used that there is no problem without a solution. In the end all of us had to find solutions.'

Cyril Ramaphosa also believed: 'There was this drive to find agreement, to find consensus, because the alternative was going to be far worse.'

While the negotiators from the main parties felt relief that intractable problems could be referred to 'the Channel', the mechanism was criticised by the smaller political parties, who felt that they were being excluded from the process and pushed to the sidelines.

While these political battles were being fought inside

1 Nelson Mandela paying a visit to the drafters at the Arniston *bosberaad*. © *Hassen Ebrahim / Constitutional Assembly*

2 Cyril Ramaphosa, Hassen Ebrahim, Nelson Mandela and Leon Wessels with the administrative team at Arniston. © *Hassen Ebrahim / Constitutional Assembly*

3 Cyril Ramaphosa and Roelf Meyer deep in conversation in Parliament. © *Avusa*

# A march on the Constitutional Assembly

17 April
1996

21 days to
deadline

Parliament, key issues of contention were unfolding outside of the building. A great deal of lobbying by interest groups had begun. In particular, the private sector and the unions faced their own showdown over the property and lock-out clauses. Business demanded a meeting with the ANC, NP and DP to express their concern about the nature of the property clause, which they believed did not protect property rights adequately. 'Business fears that investment and growth may be inhibited if property rights are not adequately protected,' said a spokesman from the South African Chamber of Business.

Cosatu, on the other hand, lobbied hard around the lock-out clause. The right of employers to lock out striking workers was a highly emotive issue for workers and the union threatened a national strike if the proposed clause was included. South Africa's largest trade union federation was happy to push this issue to the limit. The ANC backed Cosatu while other parties, supported by business, argued for the inclusion of the employer's right in some form. Tensions ran high. The different interest groups kept in touch hourly with what was happening behind closed doors in respect of the controversial clauses. As Dene Smuts noted, 'We all knew, day by day, morning by morning, afternoon by afternoon, which word was in, which word was out and who was influencing the process.'

On 17 April, Ramaphosa accepted a petition from the thousands of chemical workers who had marched to the Constitutional Assembly to present their rejection of the lock-out clause. A similar march was held the next day by members of the National Education Health and Allied Workers' Union. After receiving the memorandum from the workers, Ramaphosa spoke into a loudhailer: 'The Memorandum comes at a time when we are about to reach the final stages of completing the constitution. As I stand before you now, the Constitutional Committee is meeting, discussing some of the very issues that you are setting out in your Memorandum. It is debating the very issue of this right to strike and the right to lock-out.'

The NP and other opposition parties believed that the ANC was bowing to Cosatu's pressure and that this interfered with negotiations. The NP's Ray Radue commented: 'The tremendous pressure from labour and particularly from Cosatu, who lived around these precincts for the last three weeks, was a factor which played heavily on the ANC. I think they realised that big business was entitled, to an extent, to be protected and, at the same time, Cosatu was adamant that the lock-out would not be included in the constitution.' On the other hand, Willie Hofmeyr of the ANC believed that the pressure came from all quarters, not just the unions: 'I think, given the particular circumstances in our country, there was a lot of pressure from business, that they wanted some recognition of a balance in the constitution and equally there was a lot of pressure from the unions.'

Both Roelf and Cyril kept smiling and telling journalists that consensus would be reached. But in retrospect Ramaphosa described the final phase of negotiations as being 'marked by anxiety and great fatigue'. For the first time, he admitted that the process resembled the tension-filled days before the 1994 elections. Violence was less the issue this time. It was more a fear that a final constitution would not be achieved that would once and for all reverse the injustices and inequalities of apartheid. 'As the days grew fewer – first ten days, then seven, then four, then two – the negotiations moved from one structure to another in the hope that somewhere else a breakthrough would be achieved … In this manner, edging forward in painstakingly, barely discernible steps, the negotiations continued through the days and the nights.' As the hours ticked by, Parliament was turned into a

makeshift home for the negotiators. Couches were used for beds. A small team of dedicated Parliamentary staff led by the head waitress, Mrs R Smit, provided tea, coffee and sandwiches every two hours. Fast-food outlets brought in meals around the clock. Party caucuses were convened regularly to obtain fresh mandates. Bilateral, multilateral and sub-committee meetings took place throughout the day and night. During apartheid, Parliament had accommodated all-night sessions but, as Colin Eglin remarked, *'In the old days in this House, the all-night sittings were of a completely different nature. That was just filibustering by the opposition to keep the show going, so that the Opposition could claim that "We've taught the Government a lesson. We've made them sit all night." These late-night sittings for the Constitution were of a different order: to strike a deal and to conclude business.'*

Indeed, in these sessions, the atmosphere was electric. Journalists and observers kept watch alongside politicians, advisors and administrative staff of the Constitutional Assembly until the very end. South Africa held its breath.

**1** Cosatu march against the lock-out clause.
© William Matlala / Africa Media Online

# The final countdown

1

**1** Exhausted members of the Constitutional Assembly during the final stages of
the writing of the constitution. © *Subash Jeram / Constitutional Assembly*

# Deadlock

2

By now, newspapers and radio stations were issuing daily reports of the unfolding events in the Constitutional Assembly. The nation was gripped. On 26 April, AM Live announced to the nation:

*'Constitutional Assembly sub-committees are to continue negotiations today on the nearly 300 proposed amendments to the constitution to be filed with the Assembly this afternoon. Parties may hold closed-door negotiations throughout the weekend if necessary. Most of the amendments are technical, but several deal with substantive changes to the sections dealing with education, language, property rights and the rights of striking workers.'*

In addition, the NP was still pushing for the continuation of some form of the Government of National Unity. As Valli Moosa remarked:

*'The National Party pursued it even up to that point. They said that there should be some sort of way in which minority parties participate in the decision-making of cabinet. We told them in no uncertain terms that our mandate was to establish a full-blown democracy and there was no way in which, beyond the interim period, we would agree to any such arrangement.'*

**1** Cyril Ramaphosa briefing the media after a breakthrough in the negotiation process. © *Subash Jeram / Constitutional Assembly*

**2** A worried Cyril Ramaphosa and Roelf Meyer talking to other members of the Constitutional Assembly on the staircase in Parliament. © *Subash Jeram / Constitutional Assembly*

## Sunday 28 April 1996

10 days to deadline

Behind closed doors, parties were worried that these substantive issues were becoming intractable. For the first time there was now doubt that the constitution would be adopted by 8 May 1996. Mandela and De Klerk agreed to an urgent bilateral meeting at Mandela's Pretoria residence that Sunday.

Roelf Meyer has commented how working under the glare of the media made these bilateral sessions very different from those at Codesa.

*'At Kempton Park, Cyril and I were prepared to take decisions and take it back to our respective principles – Mr De Klerk and Mr Mandela. Now the process was far more open and transparent and whatever we did here was immediately available to those who had concerns about what sort of agreements we were going to make. So one had to interact all the time. Of course, that put a lot of pressure on those involved.'*

After ten hours of discussion between the NP and the ANC, the two main parties were joined by delegations from both Cosatu and business to discuss the property and lock-out clauses. Ramaphosa came away from the meeting stating that he was '1000 per cent sure of adopting the Constitution on May 8'. His confidence was based on significant agreements on the education, official languages and lock-out clauses reached that day. Looking back later, Ramaphosa realised that he may have been overly optimistic:

*'I got out of that meeting feeling fairly upbeat. I thought that a sound basis had been laid to resolve nearly all the difficult matters and, as it turned out, it was a false start. It was a false consensus and I almost felt like there was a little bit of egg on my face, but because we had laid a sound basis for continuing the talks, I quietly and silently in my heart thought that we will be able to resolve the problems.'*

There were other obstacles besides the false starts. The smaller parties, which were not part of the meeting with the President and Deputy President, voiced their great frustration.

1

2

The ACDP's Kenneth Meshoe said: *'I would say it is almost not democratic because … it looked like what we did throughout the months and the years before was pushed aside to finally allow what the major political parties wanted.'*

According to Constand Viljoen, *'Since Arniston the process has started looking increasingly chaotic and is no longer conducive to constitution-making.'*

Ramaphosa assured the smaller parties that nothing was finalised. Many hours of further discussion clearly lay ahead.

# The Cosatu strike

A crisis loomed as Cosatu refused to abandon its plan for a national strike, scheduled to take place the following day. Further to-ing and fro-ing on the education and property clauses continued. The possibility that the constitution might not be finished was becoming very real. A frustrated chairperson told the NP: *'We are now bending over backwards here, when your colleagues inside there are not bending over backwards to do anything. I mean we are in deep shit here, to be frank with you. We had a signed and sealed deal on Sunday. We've already had to reopen it. We are now going to have to go back again.'*

The issues remained the same. The ANC would not agree to single-medium education, which it saw as an attempt to continue white privilege. For Blade Nzimande, the ANC's chief negotiator on education, *'to constitutionally entrench single-medium and clearly Afrikaans schools would have entrenched one of the relics of apartheid forever. It was a choice between an apartheid and a democratic South Africa. The bottom lines were very clear'*. Roelf Meyer was equally adamant. He insisted to the assembled press after an NP caucus, *'Where a school has students that all speak a specific language, a school should not be forced to cater for other languages of a dual or parallel nature.'* The NP was clearly under pressure from its white constituency.

The frustrations were starting to show even between the two most consummate negotiators.

Cyril Ramaphosa: *'The concession we made on education at Sunday's meeting must be seen to be the very last. The ANC is not in a position to go any further than that.'*

Roelf Meyer: *'We hear what you're saying, that this is more or less your bottom line. We respect that, but on the other hand you have to have an understanding that we also have particular requirements ...'*

Cyril Ramaphosa: *'I see the constitution being torpedoed on this one. I don't think we are going to adopt a constitution, quite frankly, if both of us still hold on to our positions.'*

Tensions reached fever pitch. Negotiators felt stretched to their limits. *'At a personal level, I was dreading that we might be heading for a deadlock over this issue because then I was going to be the only ANC negotiator who is left with an issue. I would say that it was one of the most difficult periods that I've gone through as a politician, frankly,'* admitted a tired Blade Nzimande. Great commitment was required all round: 'We had situations where individuals also started to pull back and say, "Now I've almost had enough." It was under those circumstances that we had to renew every effort and put in everything.'

It was agreed that further meetings would have to be convened. At lunchtime, trade union members gathered outside Parliament during the Cosatu strike. The Constitutional Committee met briefly but then adjourned. This pattern continued into the night as haggling came to nothing.

702 Eye-witness News with Andrew Bolton: *'Fears that the Rand would be hurt by Cosatu's strike have not materialised. At the same time Cosatu claims a good turnout for its strike but estimates are that it was nowhere near as big as it could have been. Cosatu was protesting to stop the inclusion of a clause in the constitution that would allow employers to lock out striking workers.'*

**1** Cyril Ramaphosa, President Mandela, Deputy President FW de Klerk and Roelf Meyer meeting the press after an urgent day-long meeting at the President's residence, 28 April 1996. © *Robert Botha*

**2** Cyril Ramaphosa addressing strikers outside Parliament. © *Subash Jeram / Constitutional Assembly*

## Tuesday
## 30 April
## 1996

8 days to
deadline

Adverts with the countdown to 8 May started to appear in all national newspapers. Given the precariousness of the negotiations, administrators crossed their fingers and hoped that there would be a constitution to present to the nation. Much later Ramaphosa commented to journalists: *'I was confident right from the start that we were going to meet our deadline and also reach agreement. That is why I suppose they used to call me "Comrade Breakthrough". I would continuously say we are going to get through it. I was so convinced of victory and ending this process on a positive basis. That confidence derived from the fact that there was just too much at stake, for all parties. I didn't even have a moment of doubt.'*

**1** Cosatu's Secretary-General, Sam Shilowa, during the strike. © *Subash Jeram / Constitutional Assembly*

# 'The centre may not hold'

**2**

On 1 May the Constitutional Committee began debating outstanding issues at two in the afternoon, and ended at five the next morning, without reaching success. At this point there were real concerns that the Constitution would not be adopted on 8 May. According to Ramaphosa, *'We are now in a danger zone. If we take a wrong turn in the next 24 hours, we could do something that we could regret for many months, possibly years.'*

Ramaphosa, Meyer and the smaller parties believed that if the deadlocked issues had to be resolved in a referendum, this would undermine the entire negotiation process.

*'If we ever go down that route, there are a number of implications for our country, economy, race relations, reconciliation. All sorts of things will start to become undone. The centre may not hold ... I don't believe we sat here for two years wasting our time, to go for a referendum,'* said Cyril Ramaphosa.

Roelf Meyer agreed: *'A referendum would not have been good for the NP and it certainly would not have been good for the ANC ... we are looking at agreeing on this constitution through consensus rather than to fight it out in terms of voting on it or, even worse, going to a referendum.'*

Colin Eglin added his perspective: *'The ANC wanted to avoid having a referendum because it would show that they had failed while the smaller opposition parties wanted to avoid having a referendum because they would have ended up with a worse constitution.'*

Other negotiators were ready to resort to a referendum as they believed it was an important negotiating tactic. For Valli Moosa, *'If they thought that we would avoid a referendum at all costs, then it would have meant that we would have been forced into making unjustifiable compromises on what were very key transformation questions.'*

Said Sheila Camerer, *'What's interesting about this phase is to see the National Party resolute at long last. On the single issue of education, they are displaying the kind of resolve which, had they displayed in respect of a few others that are not going to come out right, would have produced different results.'*

In the midst of all this, the negotiators still had the capacity to laugh. During several breaks, Cyril broke into a song by Louis Armstrong that he had been taught by Joe Slovo during Codesa. Together, they had crafted alternative words relating to the negotiations.

*'We latched on to it as a real theme song to fulfil the dreams of our people. It kept us going during the Kempton Park negotiations and I was rather pleased to have it transposed into this process and to get a few people to sing along. It was wonderful to lighten things up a bit,'* enthused a smiling Ramaphosa.

Cyril: *'Give me a kiss to build a dream on. In my imagination ...'*

Leon: *'I didn't know he had such a nice voice. He's very good actually.'*

All: *'Give me a kiss to build a dream on and my imagination will thrive upon that kiss ...'*

Cyril: *'Give us a deal to build a nation on and our imagination will make that moment live. Give us a deal to build a dream on.'*

**1** Hassen Ebrahim, Cyril Ramaphosa and Leon Wessels. Executive Director, Chairperson and Deputy Chairperson of the Constitutional Assembly, at 3 am in the morning in the final moments, with Cyril reading a joke definition of the 'organs of state'. © *Subash Jeram / Constitutional Assembly*

**2** Constitutional Assembly Chairperson, Cyril Ramaphosa, in the final stages of the process. © *Subash Jeram / Constitutional Assembly*

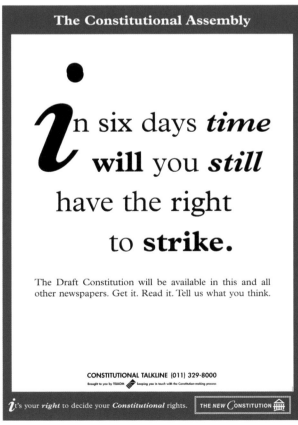

# 'Comrade Breakthrough'

2

'It's 7 o'clock on Friday 3rd May, 1996. You're listening to AM Live on SAFM 104 to 107.'

'Thank you, Sally. Good morning. The experts say, while it seems possible that agreement can be reached on the property and lock-out clauses, neither the ANC nor the National Party appeared prepared last night to back down over the education clause.

There appears to be a real prospect of the Assembly's proceedings yet again sitting into the night. There was a fourth dawn, when Assembly chairman Cyril Ramaphosa and the NP's chief negotiator emerged together, but they walked past the Assembly hall to have a well-deserved cup of tea.'

Everybody was waiting for 'the Channel' to appear with some way to break the deadlock or find a way forward. Blade Nzimande expressed the feelings of many of the negotiators: 'Relief now was that everything had been referred to the Cyril-Roelf Channel to tie down these issues.'

For Colin Eglin, 'It was inevitable that the big players had to go and do some eye-ball to eye-ball, in order to resolve their differences and to that extent, the smaller players like ourselves were less relevant.'

Roelf Meyer later recalled the pressure the Channel experienced at this time: 'Cyril and myself were sitting out here on the steps of the lobby of this room and I think we were saying to each other, "Now we have problems" because we could see there's a hesitancy to move forward.'

Saturday
4 May
1996

4 days to
deadline

**The Constitutional Assembly**

*i*n five days *time* will **women** have equal *rights?*

The Draft Constitution will be available in this and all other newspapers. Get it. Read it. Tell us what you think.

CONSTITUTIONAL TALKLINE (011) 329-8000
Brought to you by TELKOM keeping you in touch with the Constitution-making process

*i*t's your *right* to decide your *Constitutional* rights. | THE *NEW* CONSTITUTION

**The Constitutional Assembly**

*i*n four days *time* **find** out how much *power* **provincial** government *will* get.

The Draft Constitution will be available in this and all other newspapers. Get it. Read it. Tell us what you think.

CONSTITUTIONAL TALKLINE (011) 329-8000
Brought to you by TELKOM keeping you in touch with the Constitution-making process

*i*t's your *right* to decide your *Constitutional* rights. | THE *NEW* CONSTITUTION

When the meeting ended at 12.30 am on 4 May, negotiators were confident that the technical refinement team could draft amendments for consideration by the political parties later in the day. Several ANC proposals had been tabled regarding the Bill of Rights, the property clause and the lock-out clause. There was now agreement on how these clauses would be formulated. Over the next 12 hours, the technical team met with each party to go through the bill chapter by chapter. The document was then sent to print.

Education remained the outstanding point on the agenda. Closed-door negotiations continued throughout the day and night. Some of the key negotiators on both sides of the fence withdrew from the process, too weary to continue the fight. Blade Nzimande had reached his limits:

'The principle in negotiations, which I learnt pretty quickly, is that in order to negotiate in good faith, you have to respect the other side. But to be quite honest, on the education issue, I couldn't help but feel that I despised the Nats because they were trying in all sorts of ways to really entrench apartheid. In that way, I preferred the Freedom Front, because they were very straight and honest with us.'

Reports on progress emerged but no finality was in fact reached. The different party caucuses fluctuated between jubilation and despair when they thought agreement had been reached, only to discover further disagreements had cropped up. Only three days remained before the country was meant to have a new constitution. Tensions were at breaking point.

The press was now urging the negotiators to complete the job they had started. *City Press* said: '*This week support, prayers and sheer old-fashioned staying power were the request we threw at the feet of men and women writing our country's new constitution. The work has been hard. Almost back-breaking … But they have one consolation: the harder their work, the more glorious will be their triumph.*'

The media were not the only ones praying. Piet Marais recalled: '*I was sitting in my office early one of the last mornings when an old woman from Somerset West phoned. Where she got my telephone number, I don't know. She said, in Afrikaans, "When I got up this morning, something told me that I should get on my knees and pray for you particularly." Can you*

*believe it? I'm religious, but this call touched me right into my heart. I've never seen that lady. But something said to her that there is a man in Parliament who you should now phone and tell him that you're praying for him. I will never forget it.*'

Colin Eglin described the flurried activities throughout the Parliament building in these last days: '*We were scurrying around negotiating for a while and then coming back to the Assembly chamber to see what was happening with the Constitutional Committee. In one room you couldn't give away things without knowing that you were getting something in other rooms, so you actually had to orchestrate the four parallel negotiations.*'

The meetings on 6 May failed to produce any results. The atmosphere in the Constitutional Assembly was becoming acrimonious. There was no longer evidence of the consensus-seeking mode that had previously characterised much of the process. The parties were playing hardball. Once again, fatigue was a major issue. In the words of Ray Radue, '*You must remember that we had had a week in which we hardly went to bed before three in the morning and we went right through the night twice. In that situation, your body cries out for sleep and tempers become frayed and there's the pressure of knowing that time was running out. All these factors made the process extremely difficult in those last 48 hours.*'

Tuesday
7 May
1996

2 days to
deadline

**The Constitutional Assembly**

*i*n two days *time* have **all** your questions about *gun* control **answered.**

The Draft Constitution will be available in this and all other newspapers. Get it. Read it. Tell us what you think.

CONSTITUTIONAL TALKLINE (011) 329-8000

Brought to you by TELKOM keeping you in touch with the Constitution-making process.

*i*t's your *right* to decide your *Constitutional* rights. THE *NEW* CONSTITUTION

While the political parties were urgently engaged in bilateral and multilateral meetings, the IFP met elsewhere in the Parliament building to prepare its case as to why it would continue to boycott the adoption of the constitution. For the IFP, the draft constitution was still a recipe for a 'totalitarian autocracy'. *'This Bill has been described by the chairman as the birth certificate of a new nation, while on a more attentive analysis it is the advanced death certificate of pluralism, federalism, and freedom of a country which, constitutionally speaking, is committing suicide by instalments.'*

The Freedom Front, meanwhile, was locked in its own dilemma. According to Corné Mulder, *'After a discussion that went through the night, we took the decision that while there are certain positive things that we would like to support, there are other things that we cannot support.*

*In terms of what our constituency expects, we cannot be seen to support the education clause, the Preamble and some of the other issues. Those made us take the decision to abstain from the process.'* The ANC was highly disappointed. The party felt it had gone out of its way to address the FF's concerns throughout the process.

After multiple stops and starts, the Constitutional Assembly eventually resumed its debate at 5.30 pm. Finally, at 10.45 pm. the committee members began to emerge. According to Hassen Ebrahim, *'For most of us it was no different to the experience of an expectant parent waiting to see a newborn after a long and difficult labour.'*

Blade Nzimande announced that he was able to present a clause that 'once and for all closed the chapter on apartheid education in the country'. Resolution was reached by including single-medium institutions as one of the alternatives to be considered by the state in securing people's right to be taught in one's home language or the language of one's choice. After a last further compromise amendment by the DP, the clause was accepted by all parties.

Next, Willie Hofmeyr's amendment to the lock-out clause, which involved deleting the provision from the Bill of Rights, was generally accepted. The DP objected, as did the NP. Roelf Meyer stated, 'We will oppose it, but not to the extent that we will vote against the constitution.' The chairperson confirmed the amendment.

Lastly, Dullah Omar reported on the controversial property clause. The proposed amendment ensured that those who owned property would not be arbitrarily deprived of their assets while at the same time the new clause recorded the need for land reform.

The parties had reached a settlement. It was 12.30 pm. There were no longer days to the deadline but, rather, hours. Some analysts contend that for the opposition parties these final resolutions were less about seeking consensus than about suspending their demands and that the NP simply 'surrendered' Afrikaner sovereignty at this point. Some go so far as to say that 'De Klerk's negotiators were really a part of Mandela's team in facilitating the transition to majority rule. It was a pushover.' But the key NP negotiators view this moment very differently. For Leon Wessels, 'it was our common South Africanness' that had triumphed. For Roelf Meyer, the accusation that the Afrikaners meekly handed over power when the chips were down could not have been further from the reality.

'We have succeeded in bringing democracy to South Africa and that was the overall determining objective. There could be no real democracy if one would have tried to retain certain vetoes for minorities whatever the case may be.'

Ramaphosa was very moved. 'Members of the Constitutional Committee argued, differed and fought but I also saw them embracing at 3.00 am when we reached agreement on a matter which most of us thought we would never reach. I saw tears in their eyes, and I know that they were a group of people who would indeed deliver a constitution to this country. I thank them most sincerely.'

**The Constitutional Assembly**

*t*omorrow find out if *you* have the **right** to *freedom* of **speech.**

The Draft Constitution will be available in this and all other newspapers. Get it. Read it. Tell us what you think.

CONSTITUTIONAL TALKLINE (011) 329-8000

Brought to you by TELKOM  Keeping you in touch with the Constitution-making process

*i*t's your **right** to decide your *Constitutional* rights.   THE *NEW* CONSTITUTION

# Wednesday
# 8 May
# 1996

Deadline day

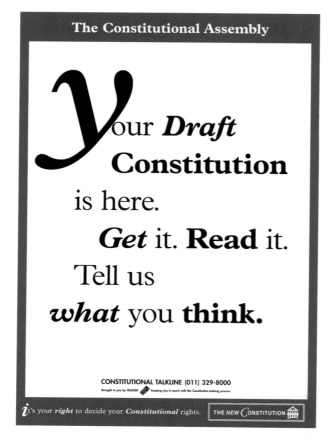

**The Constitutional Assembly**

**Y**our *Draft* **Constitution** is here. ***Get*** it. **Read** it. Tell us *what* you **think.**

CONSTITUTIONAL TALKLINE (011) 329-8000
Brought to you by TELKOM keeping you in touch with the Constitution-making process

*i*t's your *right* to decide your *Constitutional* rights.   THE *NEW* CONSTITUTION

The eighth of May was a grey, wintry day in Cape Town. Outside the Parliament building, television crews jostled for the best positions and buses of schoolchildren arrived from all over the city to bear witness to the moment. Inside the chamber, the excitement was palpable. Mandela watched in silence as the chairperson read out the Preamble and presented the Constitution to the Assembly's members.

'Today is a day of joy. It is a day of celebration. It is indeed a historic day. It is the birthday of the South African rainbow nation. This is the day when South Africa is truly born.

Since we embarked on the formal constitution-making process 24 months ago, South Africans from across the country have embraced the process as their own. It is no exaggeration when we say that a team of 43 million people worked on this Constitution.

Today we will vote on this Constitution. We will be exercising an awesome responsibility. It is my duty as chairperson to urge all of us in this Assembly, even those who may have some reservations, to vote today for a democratic and free South Africa. Let us all give our country its true birth certificate. The people of our country expect no less of us.'

FW de Klerk struck a somewhat more cautious, albeit supportive, note when he spoke: 'It is not a perfect constitution, but it is a reasonable starting point. The NP will, therefore, vote for this Constitution ... irrespective of its many shortcomings ... because it contains and enshrines many important principles with which we fully identify. Nonetheless, it was a difficult decision.'

In response to the Constitution Bill, Thabo Mbeki gave his now famous, 'I am an African' speech expressing his multiple identities as African. Thereafter voting began. A miscount meant that the voting process had to be repeated twice. At 11 am, exactly ten hours after the negotiators had tabled the last amendments, the Constitutional Assembly adopted the Constitution. The ANC, NP, DP and PAC all voted in favour; the ACDP voted against; the CP and FF abstained; while the IFP boycotted the proceedings. The combined 421 votes in favour were more than the 327 needed to make up a two-thirds majority. The ANC erupted into song as President Mandela stepped up to the podium:

'The brief seconds when the majority of honourable members quietly assented to the new basic law of the land have captured, in a fleeting moment, the centuries of history that the South African people have endured in search of a better future.'

1

2

**1** The unveiling of the Constitution mural outside Parliament. © *Subash Jeram*

**2** Nelson Mandela, FW de Klerk and the Chairperson of the Constitutional Assembly address the gathered Constitutional Assembly, members of Parliament and members of the public. © *Subash Jeram / Constitutional Assembly*

1

# Constitutional Assembly

## Republic of South Africa

## Constitution of the
Republic of South Africa
1996

### As adopted by the Constitutional Assembly on 8 May 1996

B34A – 96

ISBN 0 – 620 – 20250 – 5

**O**ne *law* for one *nation*.

# Lessons from the negotiating table

In the months after the Constitutional Assembly had adopted the Constitution, negotiators had time to sit back and reflect on what they had achieved. What did they think about the Constitution?

'I don't think it is flawless. I don't think it is without any mistakes. Given the time that we had to draft and finalise the Constitution, I think we did very, very well.' - Cyril Ramaphosa

'This document was more than a Constitution. It really was a settlement that brought South Africa together for the first time. We could really say, "Now we have one common law that unites us."' - Roelf Meyer

'There are very creative things that are there that are unusual. The extent to which we are protecting gay rights, our approach to socio-economic rights and the question of the application of the Bill of Rights – that it's not just the question of the relationship between the state and the individual, but also it governs relationships amongst individuals. Of course it's not an ANC Constitution.' - Blade Nzimande

'We would have liked the Constitution to go further in the question of expanding provincial powers, but other than that, on the governance side, it's done extraordinarily well.' - Colin Eglin

What accounted for the success of the process?

'1. We learned that, first and foremost, it was important never to let go of your dream. The participants ought to believe that a solution is possible and obstacles can be overcome …
'2. We realised that you cannot beat your negotiating partner into submission. You must have the maturity to compromise.
'3. We also learned that one should be open at all times and give our constituencies as much information as possible.' - Leon Wessels

'The DP were dubbed the '1.7% Party'. In terms of the number of votes we had no power. I think that's where the skill of negotiating comes in. I had a very simple rule. If you wanted anything in the Constitution, you had to sell it to the ANC. If you wanted anything out of the Constitution, you had to persuade the Nats to block it. At times, you had to go to the media, let them bat on that particular issue. You always had to ask, "In addition to charm and intellectual arguments, how can you have more clout?"' - Colin Eglin

'The Constitution was drafted by first negotiating areas of potential agreement … which gave parties the confidence to buy into the Constitution as a whole … Over time negotiators began to learn to separate their political differences from their growing respect for each other as people. They learnt how to laugh together and at each other … During their darkest moments, negotiators never failed to find something to make light of the moment … the negotiations succeeded not simply out of compromise but because individuals from opposing ends of the political spectrum were able to trust each other and guide the conflict-ridden country through its stormiest waters.' - Hassen Ebrahim

**1** The final Constitution as adopted by the Constitutional Assembly, 8 May 1996.
© Constitutional Assembly

'For me, the driving force throughout the negotiations was the phenomenal inspiration one had from being part of a great movement that was the ANC. The organisation had great clarity on policy, on the demands, and on the ultimate strategic objective of having a democratic South Africa that would be non-racial and non-sexist. Armed with all that, I just felt that we couldn't go wrong. We were also driven by the sense that we couldn't fail. I kept saying to myself, "What would we say to the founders of this movement in 1912 who had done so much that finally we are the generation that failed? How would we explain to our people that we were given this task to deliver this final blow and that we had failed?"' - Cyril Ramaphosa

## There were many frustrations.

'It can be terribly frustrating and very tiring and extremely boring at times, but I do enjoy the cut and thrust of it, the process of trying to find solutions. It is a real intellectual challenge. So I think while you're in it you often get very frustrated and tired and upset even, but I think when you take a more bird's-eye view, you have a much greater sense of achievement.' - Willie Hofmeyr

## What were the highlights of the process?

'Working so closely with the political representatives as we did, the administration learnt a great deal. In this regard, I believe that all of us developed the greatest respect for our chairpersons. The quality of their leadership and the brilliance of mind was a source of continuous inspiration to all.

Without their leadership, it would have never been possible to deliver this Constitution and engage the vast majority of our people in the way we have done.' - Administration team

'I think the real jewel in the crown is our Bill of Rights. We put affirmative action as a constitutional principle in a Bill of Rights to provide redress for the past. We have economic and social rights in the Constitution, thus resolving the silly debate that only traditional political rights can be legally protected. We have provisions which are unique, like the right to information as a constitutionally protected right.' - Kader Asmal

'The process of writing South Africa's Constitution will remain for a long time. It was not easy for me as an African woman to make my own voice heard on behalf of the women who could never come and speak here, so one had to really make the best of it and I really regard myself as having been honoured and very lucky to participate in it.' - Baleka Mabete-Kgositsile

'I wouldn't like to do it for my living, but to go into it for a kind of concerted period was very exciting. I mean you have to keep on reminding yourself just how important the decisions are that you're involved with. It's not just an ordinary negotiations process. It really is something that's going to shape the country for the next century or two, hopefully.' - Willie Hofmeyr

'I am personally very glad that I had the opportunity to spend full-time on the constitution-making exercise from the National Party's point of view. One feels that you almost didn't exist during that period, but it was all worth it. Personally, if I look back, I think that was the only way to do it. We could have drawn it out for longer but we would not have achieved a better result, I'm quite sure.' – Roelf Meyer

'There was magic in the air throughout the process. We were witnessing and involved in something that was far, far above us. The birth of a new nation. I feel so privileged to have been part of this process. It does not always happen in one's lifetime that you are given this unbelievable opportunity and at a young age.' – Cyril Ramaphosa

Apartheid was finally put to bed. The negotiation process both at Kempton Park and in the Constitutional Assembly had set the stage for the National Party to apologise for the past:

'Apartheid was wrong. I apologise in my capacity as leader of the NP to the millions who suffered wrenching disruption of forced removals … Who over the years suffered the shame of being arrested for pass law offences. Who over the decades and indeed centuries suffered the indignities and humiliation of racial discrimination … This apology is offered in a spirit of true repentance, in full knowledge of the tremendous harm that apartheid has done to millions of South Africans.' – FW de Klerk before the Truth and Reconciliation Commission

'I am now more convinced than ever that apartheid was a terrible mistake that blighted our land. South Africans did not listen to the laughing and the crying of each other. I am sorry that I had been so hard of hearing for so long.' – Leon Wessels

The next hurdle for the weary drafters was for the Constitutional Court to certify the Constitution and ratify that it complied with the 34 Constitutional Principles. This was to prove another lengthy and thrilling chapter in the constitution-making exercise.

# Certifying One Law for One Nation

## July-December 1996

'The Constitutional Court of South Africa was established because of the unique and painful history of our country. The court had to be the guardian of the fundamental rights enshrined in the new Constitution. In carrying out its function to first certify and then interpret the Constitution, it had to point the way with regard to the new direction chosen by the people of South Africa.'

Chief Justice Pius Langa

1

**1** President Mandela congratulates Deputy
Chairperson of the Constitutional Assembly,
Leon Wessels, on the work he did for the
Constitution. © *Robert Botha*

**2** President of the Constitutional Court, Arthur
Chaskalson, with President Mandela at the
Constitutional Court, Braamfontein, 4 August
1998. © *Robert Botha / Business Day*

# The Certification of the Final Constutution

## Overview

One of President Mandela's first tasks after his inauguration was the appointment of the 11 new Constitutional Court justices. This act was highly significant. Throughout apartheid, the judiciary had been overwhelmingly male and white and was perceived as being complicit in implementing some of the worst abuses of that period. The new Court promised a completely new judicial era. Within a day of its inauguration, the court heard one of its most controversial cases – the question of the constitutionality of the death penalty. Many groups opposed the Court's judgement declaring the death penalty unconstitutional, but the credibility of the justices was never questioned. The Court was universally commended for its conduct and its independent and forthright stance.

Just over a year later, on 10 May 1996, the Constitutional Court received another formidable task – to certify the newly adopted Constitution. According to the Interim Constitution, the new Constitution was 'not of any force and effect unless the Constitutional Court has certified that all the provisions of such text comply with the Constitutional Principles'. It was now up to this new court to decide if the draft did indeed comply with the 'solemn pact' of the 34 principles that had been hammered out by the political parties in the heat of the negotiations.

Such an assignment for a court was without precedent anywhere in the world. Advocate George Bizos, the man who would argue the Constitutional Assembly's case for the Court to certify the draft text, believed that the unusual procedure had been designed 'to pacify the minority parties which feared the previously disenfranchised voters might treat them as the oppressed had been treated for almost four centuries'. For the minority parties, the Constitutional Principles and the Court's role provided a psychological safeguard that enabled them to 'give up power'.

Other commentators believed that it was the precarious circumstances in which the negotiators found themselves during Codesa and MPNP that forced them to agree to the new Constitutional Court having the final say. For the people around the table, the peaceful settlement of South Africa's future was at stake.

The Court was all too aware of the risks when the certification hearing began in July 1996. Fortunately, it had already established itself as a strong, independent and important institution in the new democracy. The Court also went out of its way to invite public participation in the certification case by asking for written objections to the Constitution. Political groups that had hitherto stayed aloof from the constitutional process, as well as many civil society organisations and individuals, became directly engaged in the new constitutional order.

The hearing lasted two weeks and traversed a wide range of issues from the provisions of the Bill of Rights, to language rights, the rights of traditional leaders and the allocation of powers between national and provincial governments. The Court's decision not to certify the Constitution in this first round was heralded as an important milestone in the country's development as a constitutional democracy. The Constitutional Court passed the constitution in the second certification case. In the words of President Chaskalson: *'Constitutional adjudication was established as an effective partner in the transformation envisioned by the Constitution in our new democracy'.*

2

# A new court for a new nation

June
1994

Two months after South Africa's first democratic elections, President Mandela appointed Arthur Chaskalson as the first President of the Constitutional Court. He did so in consultation with the Cabinet and with Michael Corbett, Chief Justice of the time. Chaskalson had been integral to the process of writing the Interim Constitution and, with his strong track record in human rights law, was eminently suited to lead the Court. In accordance with the agreement reached during the heated MPNP negotiations, Mandela also appointed the first four justices from the ranks of the Supreme Court: Justices Laurie Ackermann, Richard Goldstone, Tholie Madala and Ismail Mohammed.

The remaining six justices were appointed after a gruelling process of interviews before the Judicial Service Commission (JSC), an independent body made up of justices, legal professionals and members of Parliament. Twenty-five people, out of an original list of a hundred nominees, were interviewed. The interviews were conducted in a theatre in Johannesburg with the media and public present. This signalled a decisive break from the past when judges were appointed in secret. The members of the JSC sat on the stage while those being interviewed sat at a small table facing them. The public occupied the seats behind the candidate. Kate

O'Regan, one of the candidates, who was ultimately successful, recounts: '*The interview was somewhat daunting. The theatre was quite dark and one did have a sense of being "in the spotlight". I supported the new process as an important mechanism for judicial accountability.*'

Following the interviews, the JSC submitted a list of ten candidates to President Mandela. Again in consultation, Mandela confirmed the final six justices. They were Justice John Didcott, Justice Johann Kriegler, Advocate Pius Langa, Professor Yvonne Mokgoro, Associate Professor Kate O'Regan and Professor Albie Sachs. The justices were to serve a single, non-renewable term of seven years, which was later extended to 12 years. In 2001, the positions of President of the Constitutional Court and Chief Justice were merged.

**1** Justices of the Constitutional Court with President Mandela and Minister of Justice, Dullah Omar, at the inauguration of the Constitutional Court, 14 February 1995. © *Robert Botha / Business Day*

**2** The 11 Justices of the Constitutional Court. Back row, left to right: Justice Madala, Justice Sachs, Justice Ackermann, Justice Yacoob (appointed 1998), Justice O'Regan, Justice Ngcobo, Justice Goldstone. Front Row, left to right: Justice Kriegler, Deputy President Langa, President Chaskalson, Justice Mokgoro. © *Giselle Wulfsohn*

1

Justice O'Regan offers an interesting perspective on whether the JSC fulfilled its specific mandate to select a representative judiciary: '*In 1994, there were approximately 150 justices in South Africa, of whom about 145 were white men. The first 11 justices were very diverse when compared to justices prior to 1994, though still not very diverse when compared to our national demographics.*'

O'Regan says, however, that the varied life experiences of the justices on that first court were as important as race and gender: '*One had been in exile, one had got his law degree as a prisoner on Robben Island, several had been detained as political detainees, many had acted for organisations resisting apartheid, some had had judicial experience, others had been legal professors or practitioners and never had judicial experience. Our ages also ranged widely. The breadth of background was very valuable.*'

In an official publication for the tenth anniversary of the Court, the first 11 justices reflected on the first bench: '*Motley as our lives and professional experiences had been, we quickly became a warm, collegial and united court … We all felt it a great privilege to be on the court. There can be no greater challenge and no greater pleasure for a justice than to feel part of a generation that lays the foundations of a creative, principled and operational jurisprudence of constitutional democracy that will endure.*'

# The Constitutional Court is inaugurated

**14 February 1995**

In mid-February 1995, President Mandela inaugurated South Africa's first Constitutional Court in its makeshift home in an office block in Braamfontein, Johannesburg. The inauspicious surroundings were offset by the poignancy and significance of the occasion. Mandela opened the ceremony with these moving words: *'The last time I appeared in court was to hear whether or not I was going to be sentenced to death. Fortunately for myself and my colleagues we were not. Today I rise not as an accused but, on behalf of the people of South Africa, to inaugurate a court South Africa has never had, a court on which hinges the future of our democracy.'*

Wearing specially tailored green robes with white neckties that distinguished them from the justices of the High Court, the justices took their oath of office in front of the President and the Minister of judges, Dullah Omar. The justices solemnly affirmed to uphold and protect the Constitution and the fundamental rights entrenched in it and to administer justice to all persons alike without fear, favour or prejudice in accordance with the Constitution. With six justices speaking in English, one in Afrikaans, one in both English and Afrikaans, one in IsiZulu, one in Sesotho and one in IsiXhosa, the diversity of the new court was immediately established. President Mandela ended the ceremony with a word of caution to the justices: *'Yours is the most noble task that could fall to any legal person ... The guarantee of the fundamental rights and freedoms for which we have fought so hard lies in your hands ... We expect from you, no, demand of you, the greatest use of your wisdom, honesty and good sense – no short cuts, no easy solutions.'*

The justices were well aware of the great challenges that lay ahead. They were starting with a blank slate and had to decide on issues of both principle and practice. The justices acknowledged that in this 'uncharted territory' their own particular assumptions, biases, aspirations and commitments would have a bearing on their judgements. For Justice Langa (later to become Deputy Chief Justice in 2001 and then Chief Justice in 2005), *'It was both fascinating and exhilarating to be part of this. The Court had to establish its jurisprudence, almost from scratch. This was a momentous responsibility.'*

The Court moved quickly to meet the responsibility of securing a firm and reliable judicial foundation for the new country and to generate public support for its role. Their boldness, energy and rigour were evident in their choice of the first case to be heard. On 15 February 1995, the justices took their seats to hear the case of the *State v Makwanyane*, which raised the question of the constitutionality of the death penalty. This was one of the most controversial issues ever heard by a court in South Africa, and large crowds of lawyers and observers packed the newly inaugurated courtroom for the three days of argument.

**1** Justice Goldstone watching Justice Mkgoro being sworn in. © *Avusa*

**2** Journalists visiting the gallows after the death penalty was declared unconstitutional. © *Ruvan Boshoff / Sunday Times*

In a unanimous judgement, the court ruled that the death penalty was unconstitutional. The judgement comprised 11 separate but concurring judgements. Each emphasised the value of human dignity, one of the cornerstones of the new Constitution. Justice Madala stated, 'the death penalty is a punishment which involves so much pain and suffering that civilised society ought not to tolerate it even in spite of the present high crime rate.' Justice Mokgoro added that 'even the vilest criminal remains a human being ... Central to the commitment to basic human rights is the need to revive the value of human dignity in South Africa. Life and dignity are two sides of the same coin.'

Many groups opposed this ruling, including the NP, which declared that it would campaign to have the death penalty reinstated. Others called for a referendum to gauge public opinion. Although the justices gave serious consideration to this action, President Chaskalson ultimately declared: 'The question before us is not what the majority of South Africans believe a proper sentence for murder should be. It is whether the Constitution allows the sentence.'

President Chaskalson set out the Court's duty in clear terms: 'Public opinion is no substitute for the duty vested in the courts to interpret the Constitution and to uphold its provisions without fear or favour. If public opinion were to be decisive there would be no need for constitutional adjudication. The protection of rights could then be left to Parliament which has a mandate from the public ... but this would be a return to parliamentary sovereignty and a retreat from the new legal order established by the 1993 Interim Constitution.'

Despite the unpopular judgement, the credibility of the Court and its 11 justices was never questioned, and the new court was commended for its commitment to judicial activism. For Justice Langa, 'the most important achievement was the acceptance of the Court's work by the South African people. This established the position of the judiciary, and its independence, as being a key part of the South African firmament.'

# Certification

10 May
1996

**CARMEL RICKARD** reports on the awesome challenge facing the learned people on the bench of South Africa's first Constitutional Court

## Judging the CONSTITUTION

POLITICAL POSER . . . court president Arthur Chaskalson

A year and a bit after this complex and difficult case, the Constitutional Court faced another 'massive and extraordinary task' - the certification of the Constitution. For President Chaskalson, it *was a totally unique undertaking. I don't know if any other court in the world had ever undertaken to determine if a constitution was constitutional'.*

The stakes were high. Once the Court had certified the text, the matter of compliance with the Principles could never be raised again in any court of law, including the Constitutional Court. That casts an increased burden on the Court in deciding on certification. *'Should we subsequently decide that we erred in certifying we would be powerless to correct the mistake, however manifest,'* declared the court.

For the members of the Constitutional Assembly who had spent two years drafting the Constitution, the moment of handing the draft text to the Court was equally charged. *'For those of us who were involved,'* explained Cyril Ramaphosa, *'this was the endorsement that I think we yearned for. After certification, no one could ever turn around and say, "They wrote the Constitution and that was their own doing."'*

Ramaphosa likened the certification case to a health check: *'I wanted an independent source to say, "We declare that you are healthy and it's a great constitution. Let it be released to the people of this country." You can't write your own birth certificate. Somebody had to sign it. For me, that was the moment.'*

Justice Kriegler believed that the Court approached this 'health check' with a attitude of 'consensus-mindedness'. *'The Codesa and Constitutional Assembly process had evolved a spirit of leaving thorny issues aside and getting on with consensus. Everyone was still very much in a cooperative state of mind.'*

Consensus-minded or not, the justices faced several difficult questions. What would happen if an unelected body of justices overturned the decisions of the elected representatives of the people who wrote the Constitution? Would the Court be accused of being 'counter-majoritarian' and would this lead to public rejection of the judgement? Would the highest court in the land lose its legitimacy as an institution at the very outset of its life? Would all the hard work and delicate negotiations be derailed if the South Africa's first democratic constitution wasn't certified? What would happen if individual parties chose to ignore the decision of the Court?

**1** Headline from The *Sunday Times,* 10 May 1996. © *Sunday Times*

**2** The Court's logo - a tree sheltering people sitting beneath it - is a representation of the traditional African concept of justice under a tree. It signified the protection of people's right in the new SA. © *Constitutional Court Library*

**3** Ramaphosa's letter to the Court, 10 May 1996. © *Constitutional Assembly*

By this time, the National Party had in fact left the Government of National Unity to establish itself as the main opposition party. If the party now reneged on agreements because of the new parliamentary landscape, could it bring South Africa's peaceful settlement to a premature demise? Would this in turn spark a constitutional crisis in the country?

In trying to grapple with these questions, the Court had to acknowledge that it was itself a new institution. It was still in the process of establishing its own legitimacy while also having to ensure the credibility of the Constitution. The justices could not be seen to align themselves with the ruling party. It had to be the people's constitution, not the ANC's constitution.

The Court emphasised from the outset that it held a judicial, not a political, mandate in the certification case. Even though a constitution by its very nature deals with political power, this was a legal exercise as the judgement later outlined. 'This court has no power, no mandate, and no right to express any view on the political choices made by the Constitutional Assembly, the wisdom of any provision of the [draft text] is not this court's business ...' Justice O'Regan elaborated further on this issue: *'The question was not whether a particular provision would be desirable or effective, which was the key question for the Constitutional Assembly.'*

Although the Court's mandate was clear, the challenges remained. The justices described the Constitutional Principles as 'broad constitutional strokes' that could not be interpreted with 'technical rigidity'. Given that each principle was capable of being complied with in more than one way, how was the Court going to respond to competing interpretations which were all nevertheless compliant? The justices were to spend much time pondering this issue. Justice Mohammed (later Deputy President of the Constitutional Court) put forward a useful metaphor to think about this:

*'The Constitutional Principles are the lights of the runway within which you operate the plane. You can choose the speed and the angle, but it must be between its lights.'*

The aeroplane metaphor was to recur frequently in the next weeks.

3

2

# Public submissions

## CERTIFICATION OF THE NEW CONSTITUTION BY THE CONSTITUTIONAL COURT.

1. The interim Constitution of 1993 requires the Constitutional Assembly to draft and adopt a new Constitution which must comply with the 34 Constitutional Principles set out in schedule 4 to the interim Constitution.

2. For the new Constitution to be valid and come into effect the Constitutional Court must certify that all its provisions comply with these 34 principles.

3. The Constitutional Assembly adopted a new Constitution on the 8th May 1996. The Constitutional Court has now received a request from the Constitutional Assembly to certify that this Constitution complies with the Constitutional Principles.

4. In terms of the rules of the Constitutional Court political parties represented in the Constitutional Assembly are entitled to present argument to the Court as to whether or not the Constitution should be certified.

5. The Constitutional Court has decided that anyone else wishing to object to the certification of the new Constitution on the grounds that it does not comply with the Constitutional Principles may do so subject to the following conditions:
   (a) A written objection must be lodged with the Registrar of the Constitutional Court, Forum II, Braampark, 33 Hoofd Street, Braamfontein. 2017. by not later than 3p.m. on the 31st May 1996.
   (b) The written objection must not be more than 1000 words. It must identify –
      (i) The particular provision of or omission from the Constitution to which objection is taken.
      (ii) The grounds for the objection.
      (iii) The relevant Constitutional Principles contained in schedule 4 with which the provision or omission does not comply.

6. The written objection may be in any of the official languages and must provide the name of the objector and an address to which communications to the objector can be directed. Objectors are required to lodge 25 copies of their objection with the Registrar of the Constitutional Court and to deliver a copy of the objection to the Executive Director of the Constitutional Assembly at 9th Floor, Regis House, cnr Adderley and Church Streets, Cape Town or dispatch a copy by prepaid registered post to him at P O Box 15, Cape Town, 8000. Fax (021) 24-1160.

7. The written objection must deal only with the objector's contention that the new Constitution does not comply with the Constitutional Principles. The Constitutional Court has no jurisdiction to consider the wisdom or merit of the terms of the new Constitution and any representations made regarding such matters would be irrelevant.

8. The Constitutional Court will consider all written objections lodged with the Registrar in accordance with the provisions set out above. Should it require an objection to be amplified, or written argument to be submitted to it in support of such objection, it will give further directions to the objector concerned.

9. A special session of the Constitutional Court will be convened to hear argument in public on whether the Constitution complies with the Constitutional Principles.

10. Oral argument will be heard on behalf of the following bodies or persons provided that they comply with directions given in terms of the rules of the Constitutional Court:
   (a) The Constitutional Assembly.
   (b) Any political party represented in the Constitutional Assembly.
   (c) Any objector authorised by the Court to present oral argument to it, in terms of written directions given by it after consideration of the written objections lodged in terms of paragraph 5 hereof.

11. The public hearing will take place at the Constitutional Court, Forum II, Braampark, 33 Hoofd Street, Braamfontein. 2017. The date provisionally fixed for the commencement of the public hearing is the 1st July 1996.

A CHASKALSON
PRESIDENT CONSTITUTIONAL COURT.

Mirroring the Constitutional Assembly's drive for transparency and public participation, the Court extended an open invitation to all South Africans to submit objections to the Constitution. The President of the Court, intent on dealing with the matter as thoroughly and swiftly as possible, fixed 1 July 1996 as the date for commencement of the case. The case was set to last for ten days, longer than any other matter that had come before the Court.

A plethora of written submissions arrived at the court building. Eighty-four special interest groups and members of the public – ranging from the South African Police, human rights NGOs, traditional leaders, employers' associations, trade unions and campaigners for the death penalty – all lodged objections in the hope of changing the text of the final Constitution. South Africans once again demonstrated their eagerness to have their views and expectations heard.

Five of the political parties that had participated in the Constitutional Assembly also submitted written objections. Their 'yes' vote in Parliament on 8 May 1996 was obviously not an indication of their full agreement with every clause in the Constitution they had helped to write. Certification presented another opportunity to have their opinions more fully incorporated in the final text. Other parties who had stood aloof from constitution-making now decided to invest in the process. The IFP, which had stormed out of the Constitutional Assembly, seized the moment to have its voice heard. So did the Conservative Party.

In all, the court received 155 objections to the text. A special room was set aside and extra staff hired to process the 2 500 pages of submissions that piled up as well as the extracts from judgements, textbooks and other publications that were annexed.

While the content of all the submissions were taken into account, the Court ultimately afforded an audience to 27 groups. 'In deciding whom to invite to present oral argument, we were guided by the nature, novelty, cogency and importance of the points raised in the written submission ... The underlying principle was to hear the widest possible spectrum of potentially relevant views,' explained the justices in the final judgement.

1 This letter from President Chaskalson, which gave detailed instructions as to how objections should be specified, appeared in many newspapers. © Constitutional Court Library

2 One page of the summary of objections submitted as part of the certification case. © Constitutional Court

# The proceedings

## SUMMARY OF OBJECTIONS AND SUBMISSIONS ANNEXURE 3

| Objections by Private Parties Text | Objector | Subject of objection |
|---|---|---|
| Preamble | AC Cilliers | Stress on 'injustices of our past' instead of non-discrimination and reconciliation |
| Preamble | MH Prozesky | 'May God protect our people' discriminates against non-theists |
| 6(3) read with 6(4) | AC Cilliers | Use of particular official languages for the purposes of government |
| 6 and 9 | Concerned South African Indian Citizens | Non-recognition of Telegu, Gujarati, Urdu, Tamil and Hindi as official languages |
| 6 | Prince Madlakadlaka on behalf of Queen Modjadji | Non-recognition of Khilobedu as an official language |
| 6 | G Moralee | English should be the only official language |
| Ch 2 | J Anderson | Limitation of rights |
| Ch 2 | J Anderson | Sexual orientation as a ground for non-discrimination |
| Ch 2 | J Munnikhuis | Failure to make legal system more accessible and protective of the lay person and to promote position of women in law |
| Ch 2 | HW Theron | The defined rights are not adequately clarified |
| 8(2) | Gauteng Association of Chambers of Commerce and Industry | Horizontal application of the Bill of Rights |
| 8(2) | Free Market Foundation | Horizontal application of the Bill of Rights |
| 8(2) | Congress of Traditional Leaders of South Africa | Horizontal application of the equality clause will impact on indigenous law |
| 8(2) and (3) | SA Institute of Race Relations | Horizontal application of the Bill of Rights |
| 8(2) and (3) | Transvaalse Landbou-Unie | Horizontal application of the Bill of Rights |
| 8(3) | Free Market Foundation | Anomalous and creates a law-making function of the courts by making no provision for customary law |
| 8(4) | P Bond, L Zita and D Miller | Protection of rights of juristic persons |

The Constitutional Assembly appointed a team of advocates to defend the draft text. George Bizos, a leading human rights advocate who had been involved in many high-profile political cases during the apartheid regime, led a team consisting of Wim Trengove, Marumo Moerane, Nona Goso and Kgomotso Moroka. Forty-eight advocates represented the objectors, excluding the attorneys who had briefed and supported them. This was the largest number of legal professionals to be involved in a single case. *'One hundred and fifty-five issues to be heard over two weeks, with more than 50 lawyers arguing one issue after another, was a hell of an exciting and very pressurised and extraordinary thing,'* reflected Wim Trengove. *'Most extraordinary of course was that the Constitution would normally be the base rule against which everything else is measured and argued. We were now going to be debating the underlying foundation of our law. We knew at the time that this was a highly unusual, once-in-a-lifetime event.'*

George Bizos recounts how the *'five of us in our team drafted more than 250 pages of argument that we hoped would show conclusively that the constitution complied.'*

The court divided the objections into broadly associated topics that were to be heard at specific times over a period of 11 days. The lead counsels for the Assembly was afforded the right to open the debates. Each objection was then heard from individuals, representatives of organisations or political parties. The court set out in advance how much time – specified in minutes – the Constitutional Assembly and the objector had to speak. A system of three lights was introduced. A green light went on at the start of a person's time. A minute or two from the end of the allocated time, a yellow light showed. A red light indicated it was time to stop. 'You can imagine how fascinating it was, because lawyers are used to going to court and having a single issue to argue for a whole day,' commented Wim Trengrove.

1

## Christians for Truth

Private Bag 250 • Kranskop • 3268 • RSA • E-mail: 100076.620@compuserve.com
Tel: (032) 481-2512 • Fax: (032) 481-2507

May 31, 1996

The Registrar
Constitutional Court
Fax: 011 4036524

OBJECTION TO NEW CONSTITUTION

The new Constitution does not directly provide for a right of **protection of family and marriage.**
This right is universally protected by *inter alia* the following:
a) Section 12 of the Universal Declaration of Rights of the UN (1948).
b) Article 10 of the International Covenant on Economic, Social and Cultural Rights (1966).
c) Article 23(1) of the International Covenant on Civil and Political Rights (1966).
d) Articles 8(1) and 12 of the European Convention on Human Rights (1950).
e) Article 5(d)(iv) of the International Covenant on the Elimination of All Forms of Racial Discrimination (1965).
f) Part I (16) of the European Social Charter (1961).
g) Article 18 of the Banjul Charter on Human and People's Rights (1981) (The African Charter of Human Rights).
h) Article 6 of the German Basic Law (1949).
i) Article 41 of the Irish Constitution (1937).

In view of the above, it is submitted that the new Constitution must be amended to make provision for the inclusion of a right on the protection of the family and of marriage.

Yours sincerely

Rev K. Olsen
(Deputy President of CFT)

*Attached is a copy of CFT's press statement (13 May 1996) concerning the new Constitution.*

2

Dear Sir / Madam

My family I are opposed to demand. There no price on human life. Human Life is sacred in a mother's womb. and no one has right to go and murder a innocent human life. Abortion is not the way to ensure population control or to deal with what are euphemistically called unwanted pregnancies. It is the deliberate killing of an innocent human being and only God can determine when that life begins and when it ends. Life begins at conception in a mother's womb. This violence against the peacefully loving little human beings and the most innocent human life and most defenceless of our society. If there is violence in the mother's womb how can there be peace in the world. Unborn babies must get right to live and not hardened criminal who murder innocent people. Let unborn babies live.

Your's faithfully
Miss M de Barros

My Address is   50 Melbourne Road
Woodstock
7925
Cape Town

**1-4** Examples of the objections to the final
Constitution received by the Constitutional Court.
© *Constitutional Court Library*

## Protecting the Bill of Rights

The sense of public engagement with the certification process continued during the first week when a range of individuals, parties and lobby groups brought forward issues relating to the Bill of Rights. One of the most dramatic moments in the whole case unfolded with the presentation of arguments in this cluster by the Congress of Traditional Leaders of South Africa. Contralesa contended that the rights entrenched in the Bill of Rights would undermine traditional patriarchal systems and that there was no role for traditional leaders in local government.

Two of Contralesa's senior members, Inkosi Mwelo Nonkonyana and Inkosi Sango Patekile Holomisa, who were also advocates, argued the case. While they arrived in court on the morning of their appearance in suits and ties, they returned after the lunch break in their traditional ceremonial attire of animals skins, carrying shields and entering the chamber barefoot. The surprised audience wondered if they were in fact in contempt of court, as they would have been in the past. The *amakhosi* later told the media that President Chaskalson had agreed that they could appear in this way because they were acting in their capacity as traditional leaders rather than advocates. During their presentation, Justice Mokgoro, one of the two women justices, entered into a heated debate about interpretations of the custom of *ilobolo* (bridewealth) and the role of traditional law.

Advocate Moerane replied for the Constitutional Assembly. While he acknowledged the complexities of the role of traditional leaders, he argued forcefully for the right to gender equality: *'You cannot have a situation where certain people are placed beyond the protection of the Bill of Rights. Everyone is entitled to them.'*

## Administration and labour issues

The first week ended with argument dedicated to the courts and administration of justice as well as perceived problems relating to the separation of powers. In an issue that was to become highly topical over the next few years, Advocate Trengove alerted the justices to the fact that the Judicial Service Commission was likely to include a high proportion of politicians. Justice Mohammed retorted indignantly that 'The whole idea [of the JSC] was to get away from political control as in the past.' Trengove responded with an argument that would become common: *'The only issue we are concerned with is the Constitutional Principles which demand judicial independence. We say it is not necessarily an ingredient for judicial independence that there be no political input.'*

The focus moved to whether the Constitution adequately protected the independence of the Attorney-General and other watchdog bodies such as the Auditor-General and the Public Protector. The question raised was what confidence the public could have in these positions if a simple majority could fire its officials. Advocate Moerane dismissed the objection as the concern of only a single party, the DP. President Chaskalson insisted that the issue be given greater consideration. *'If officials can always be removed from office by a simple majority and do not have security of tenure, they are not independent of the majority party.'*

The passionate debate that followed cast doubt for the Constitutional Assembly team whether their arguments had found favour with the Court. 'The difficult questions that were put to members of our team did not augur well for the position we were defending,' admitted Bizos at the end of this first week. They began to suspect that the court might decide not to certify the Constitution this time round.

# Week two

**7–10 July
1996**

During the second week, objectors raised new challenges to the draft constitution while the complex philosophical and legal challenges of the first week remained the subject of further discussion and debate. The labour provisions, which had nearly scuppered negotiations, once again came under fire. Malcolm Wallis SC, acting for Business South Africa, was careful to drop the use of the phrase 'the right to lock-out' but argued essentially for the same thing - management's right to exercise economic power in pursuit of collective bargaining. This, he said, was the equivalent to the employees' right to strike, which had developed over the years into a 'most formidable weapon, capable of inflicting grievous harm on the employer'. Martin Brassey SC, acting for Cosatu, presented a cogent history of black worker disempowerment and emphasised the union's long-stated objection that this clause would entrench the age-old power of the bosses though now in the name of equal treatment.

While the justices seemed inclined to support Cosatu on the lock-out issue, they voiced strong opposition to Cosatu's request for the 'immunisation' of the Labour Relations Act of 1995 from constitutional review. The justices held that these 'justice-proof' clauses defied the principle that the court was the supreme law of the land. This, they suggested, was disturbingly reminiscent of the apartheid legal system, which had not allowed the courts to question the validity of any Act passed by Parliament. These issues occupied an entire day of argument.

The following day, the supremacy of the Constitution again emerged as an issue. The justices themselves raised concerns about the fact that a two-thirds majority could amend the Bill of Rights. Would the Bill of Rights be sufficiently protected? This led to further questions whether the core of the Constitution was safe from amendment.

The issue of the separation between the legislature and the judiciary was highlighted in a discussion on socio-economic rights as embodied in Sections 26–29 of the Constitution. Could the Court constitutionally discipline the legislature for not enacting these rights? Would this constitute a transgression of the separation of powers? These questions led to a lively debate. While the Legal Resources Centre argued for justiciable socio-economic rights, the Free Market Foundation strongly opposed them and argued for the separation of powers. The justices grappled with this complex issue:

**Justice Mohammed:** *'What must the Court do if the legislature does not take reasonable steps?'*

**Advocate Trengove:** *'The Court may then be dependent on political and public pressure to get Parliament to comply.'*

**President Chaskalson:** *'If Parliament refuses to follow a court order, there would be a constitutional crisis – the Court does not have an army.'*

**Justice Sachs:** *'My main concern is that the Court could end up usurping the role of the legislature. There is a danger that the government becomes a "dikastocracy" – rule by the justices.'*

**1** Jay Naidoo at the launch of Cosatu, Durban, 1985.
© *Paul Weinberg / Africa Media Online*

**2** Poster as part of the Constitutional Assembly media campaign.
© *Constitutional Assembly*

# The final day

The Court agreed to extend the hearings for a further day to ensure that everyone was adequately heard. Several of the advocates who had appeared in previous days in this milestone case reiterated their objections to certification going ahead. The Constitutional Assembly legal team put forward its final arguments as to why the draft text should not be sent back. The justices continued to engage individually with the issues in their lively and erudite style of debate that had characterised the entire case.

The final stages of the lengthy hearing ended, in the words of Advocate Bizos, 'with a mighty bang'. The emergency clause in the Constitution, which allowed a simple majority in Parliament to declare a state of emergency, was the last issue to be addressed. The justices felt the shadow of the past looming over the Court. George Bizos found himself in the unlikely position of having to defend the emergency clause. The irony of the situation was not lost on anyone, least of all Bizos himself. As a long-time human rights advocate, he had fought consistently for those persecuted under security and emergency legislation in the past. Bizos now had to face the indignation of the justices over issues such as inadmissible evidence, unfair trials and torture, all of which appeared possible under the emergency provision. An animated argument ensued, with Bizos 'arguing a position that was the opposite of my instincts'. Eventually Justice Kriegler suggested tactfully that the Constitutional Assembly team put in a note on the issue so that the difficult matter could be brought to a close. With that magnanimous gesture, the case came to an end. A relieved Bizos took up the aeroplane metaphor once more:

*'This is the end - or it ought to be - of a long and difficult process. There is a grave responsibility on this court to see whether the front wheel of the plane is dead centre or whether, on landing, the fringes of the wings have gone over the limits.'*

The last words went to President Chaskalson. He thanked everyone who had participated and congratulated them for the great deal of thought that had gone into their preparations. 'Now the Court has the very arduous task of discharging the mandate given to us under the Constitution,' he said.

After an exhausting 11 days of argument, the justices believed the hearing had gone extremely well. Said Justice Kriegler: *'Everyone who participated was manifestly deeply affected by this epoch-making event. The quality of the contributions was exceptional.'*

2

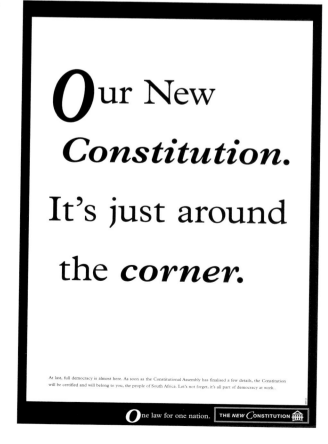

# Our New Constitution. It's just around the corner.

At last, full democracy is almost here. As soon as the Constitutional Assembly has finalised a few details, the Constitution will be certified and will belong to you, the people of South Africa. Let's not forget, it's all part of democracy at work.

One law for one nation. | THE *NEW* CONSTITUTION

# Writing the judgement

Considering the complexity of the case, it was surprising that it took just two months for the judgement to be handed down. Contrary to the death penalty case, in which each justice had written a separate judgement, this was a single decision handed down in the name of 'the Court'. After providing a detailed historical background as the backdrop to this extraordinary case, the judgement went on to record the justices' conclusions whether every particular detail contained in the new text complied or failed to comply with the stated Constitutional Principles, 'irrespective of the attitude of any interested party' as well as give reasons for each conclusion.

The justices held conferences for days on end to debate and discuss the issues among themselves and come up with a position. Various justices were then assigned different sections of the judgement to write up. Justice Kriegler was given the unenviable task of editing the judgement as a whole. *'This was the longest, the most detailed, the most diverse - not necessarily the most difficult or intellectually and emotionally tricky - but the most significant judgement I had participated in in my life. It was polished and tweaked by every one of us, but my basic job was to stitch the different sections seamlessly to ensure the same basic tone throughout. I am proud of the job we did.'*

*'What was amazing is that we got absolute consensus amongst the 11 justices,'* exclaimed **President Chaskalson.** *'This was not a small achievement given the multiplicity of cases and the massive implications of our decisions for the future.'*

# The verdict

The Court's verdict on 6 September 1996, held that although the overwhelming majority of the clauses complied with the Constitutional Principles, there were nine instances where this was not the case. These ranged from the failure to sufficiently spell out local government powers to the failure to comply with the provisions that shield an ordinary state from constitutional review. The Court held that the 'justice-proof' clauses relating to the Labour Amendment Act defied the principle that the Court was the supreme law of the land. The Court was also dissatisfied with the majorities required for amending certain sections of the Bill of Rights and with the emergency provisions. They objected to procedures for the appointment and removal of the Public Protector, the Auditor-General and the Public Service Commission.

The most contentious issue of all - that of provincial powers - dominated the judgement. About 175 of 484 paragraphs were concerned with it. The court concluded that provincial powers had been substantially reduced in the text of the 1996 Constitution in respect of provincial police powers, tertiary education, local government and traditional leadership. It deemed, however, that these were not sufficient grounds to refuse certification. But the justices found that the 'override' clause, which allowed national legislation to prevail over provincial legislation, infringed a Constitutional Principle.

These issues of non-compliance were of sufficient importance for the text to be sent back to the Constitutional Assembly. The judgement declared:

*'We are unable to and therefore do not certify that all of the provisions of the Constitution of the Republic of South Africa 1996 comply with the Constitutional Principles contained in schedule 4 to the Constitution of the Republic of South Africa Act 200 of 1993.'*

However, the judgement categorically stated that the draft text was 'a monumental achievement': *'Constitution-making is a difficult task. Drafting a constitution for South Africa, with its many unique features, is all the more difficult. Having in addition to measure up to a set of predetermined requirements greatly complicates the exercise. Yet in general and in respect of the overwhelming majority of its provisions, the Constitutional Assembly has attained that goal.'*

The Court also observed that the instances of non-compliance, although important, did not present significant obstacles to the formulation of a text that complied fully with the Constitutional Principles. Cyril Ramaphosa agreed:

*'I felt totally vindicated, because we didn't achieve a 50 per cent pass rate or even 60 per cent or 70 per cent. We actually achieved a 95 per cent pass rate. We were told exactly what we needed to do and, bingo! We knew it would be 100 per cent. We were walking on air.'*

The judgement was also heralded as a victory for constitutional democracy. The fact that none of the political parties questioned the legitimacy of the certification process or the decisions taken by the Court was an affirmation of the new democracy's commitment to the 'solemn pact'. According to Leon Wessels, *'the idea of a constitutional state was embraced emotionally by the NP for the first time when the Court declined to certify the first version of the final Constitution. That decision meant more in the minds of the supporters of the NP than anything before.'*

The Constitutional Assembly's legal team were equally pleased: *'It would have actually been a miracle if we had managed to negotiate a constitution with 250 sections which had to comply with 34 vaguely worded constitutional principles first time round ... In the bigger scheme of things, it was remarkable. The Court could also isolate the defects to make it reasonably doable for the Assembly to fix the problems.'*

Justice Kriegler reflected on how remarkably smoothly this process had run: *'This was a culmination of a process that started in the late 1980s, through to the negotiations that worked, the elections that worked, the inauguration that worked and the rugby that worked. There was this feeling that everyone was part of a collection trying to get a job done. There were differences of opinion, differences of approach, but my prevailing impression was, "Hell, this is going well."'*

**1** Justice Kriegler, President Chaskalson and Justice Sachs in the Constitutional Court. © *Gallo Images / Robbie Schneider*

# The constitution is certified, finally

## 4 December 1996

The drafters returned to Parliament. Armed with the detailed judgement and a passionate will, they had just four weeks to amend the text. Again the pressure to finish the job became intense but once more the Chairperson's optimism set the tone for the days ahead: *'What was required was very technical and it didn't really require a lot of tough work. We had got a clean bill of health and now just needed to take some vitamins and do one final test.'*

By 7 October, the job was done. It was time for Parliament to vote again. On 11 October 1996 the Constitutional Assembly approved the amended Constitution by 369 votes to one, with eight abstentions. The ACDP voted against the constitution and the Freedom Front abstained. Cyril Ramaphosa commended the drafters for what they had achieved and expressed the hope that their job was really now at an end:

*'I am not going to say goodbye because we might be referred back. I hope we are not!'*

The members of the Assembly gave the Chairperson a standing ovation. With Ramaphosa at the helm, they had achieved the impossible. They had overcome many of their deep differences, formed new relationships and drafted one of the most forward-looking constitutions in the world. With all nine problem clauses dealt with, the text was resubmitted to the Court. The same legal team was briefed. This was to be a much easier certification process.

On 18 November, the Constitutional Court began its second hearing on the amended text. Again, the general public and political parties were invited to make written representations. The issue of the power of the provinces once again dominated the agenda. The counsel for KwaZulu-Natal contended that the amended text still failed to comply with the Constitutional Principles. The Court dismissed the objection, holding that the level of detail being requested was a matter for legislation. The Court concluded that although the provinces' powers were less than those specified in the Interim Constitution, the disparity was not significant. In the final analysis the justices were unanimous that the defective provisions had been conscientiously dealt with in the amended text. On 4 December 1996, the Constitutional Court approved the Constitution of the Republic of South Africa:

*'We certify that all provisions of the amended constitutional text, the Constitution of the Republic of South Africa, 1996, passed by the Constitutional Assembly on 11 October 1996, comply with the Constitutional Principles contained in Schedule 4 of the Constitution of the Republic of South Africa, 1993.'*

At this momentous point, Advocate Bizos extended the aviation metaphor:

*'The plane was on a test flight operating on new instruments, in a manoeuvre never before attempted. Although the pilots had failed the first attempted landing, the second attempt came down successfully within the lights of the runway. It had been a bumpy ride and the Court probably didn't want to go through such an experience again, but for the negotiators the risk had paid off.'*

**1** This well-known image of the victims of the Sharpeville Massacre sent shock waves across the world. © *UWC / Robben Island Museum / Mayibuye Archives*

# South Africa's Fifth Constitution

Finally, the Constitution was ready to be signed into law. The date chosen was 10 December because it was International Human Rights Day: the place, Sharpeville, because of its historical significance. In the white town of Vereeniging just a few kilometres away, Boers and Brits had met in a bid to end the South African War, which led the way to the Union of South Africa that had disenfranchised the black majority. Fifty-eight years later, on 21 March 1960, in the township of Sharpeville, police shot dead 69 people who were peacefully protesting against the pass laws. This event had been a turning point in the history of South Africa.

The signing of the new Constitution took place in a stadium just a few metres away from where the massacre had happened. *'It was not in an air-conditioned office, a boardroom or some secret location that we did the signing. It was in a stadium, a very public place. It was an enactment of what our struggle has been all about – a very public event,'* reflected Ramaphosa.

On the day, he declared to the crowds: *'Here, at Sharpeville, in Vereeniging, both powerful symbols of past relationships between South Africans, we are making a break with the past. A break with the pain, a break with betrayal. We are starting a new chapter.'*

Mandela continued this theme in his speech to the assembled crowd: *'As we close a chapter of exclusion and a chapter of heroic struggle, we reaffirm our determination to build a society of which each of us can be proud, as South Africans, as Africans, and as citizens of the world.*

*As your first democratically elected President I feel honoured and humbled by the responsibility of signing into law a text that embodies our nation's highest aspirations. In writing the words which today become South Africa's fundamental law, our elected representatives have faithfully heard the voice of the people. Now, at last, they are embodied in the highest law of our rainbow nation.'*

All eyes were on President Mandela as the crowds waited to see the Constitution signed into law. No sooner had President Mandela put down his pen than a beaming Ramaphosa spontaneously raised the Constitution up high for the enthusiastic crowd to see.

The Constitution came into effect on 4 February 1997, replacing and repealing the Interim Constitution of 1993. At last, there was one law for one nation. Fifteen years later, Ramaphosa reminisced:

*'While watching Madiba sign the Constitution, there were a lot of emotions that went through my head. I was humbled that I was watching history unfolding. I was saying to myself, this is what it has all been about. The 69 people that died in Sharpeville, and hundreds of thousands of other people who died throughout the country, they all died to make sure that we have this document. This is the document that should wipe away the tears and the blood that was shed here and correct that horrible history.'*

1

**1** President Mandela receiving and signing the final Constitution with Chairperson Cyril Ramaphosa by his side. © *Adil Bradlow*

**2** From left to right: President Mandela greeting survivors of the *Sharpeville Massacre* during the signing ceremony. Mural of the final Constitution. President Mandela laying a wreath at the monument to the victims of the *Sharpeville Massacre*. 10 December 1996. © *Robert Botha*

1

## The Constitution

### of the Republic of South Africa, 1996

As adopted on 8 May 1996 and amended
on 11 October 1996 by the Constitutional Assembly

ISBN 0-620-20214-9

**1** South Africa's final Constitution signed by some of the
main architects involved in the constitution-making process.
© *Constitution Hill Trust*

**2** Preamble of the final Constitution. © *Constitutional Assembly*

# PREAMBLE

We, the people of South Africa,

Recognise the injustices of our past;

Honour those who suffered for justice and freedom in our land;

Respect those who have worked to build and develop our country; and

Believe that South Africa belongs to all who live in it, united in our diversity.

We therefore, through our freely elected representatives, adopt this Constitution as the supreme law of the Republic so as to –

> Heal the divisions of the past and establish a society based on democratic values, social justice and fundamental human rights;
>
> Lay the foundations for a democratic and open society in which government is based on the will of the people and every citizen is equally protected by law;
>
> Improve the quality of life of all citizens and free the potential of each person; and
>
> Build a united and democratic South Africa able to take its rightful place as a sovereign state in the family of nations.

May God protect our people.

Nkosi Sikelel' iAfrika. Morena boloka setjhaba sa heso.
God seën Suid-Afrika. God bless South Africa.
Mudzimu fhatutshedza Afurika. Hosi katekisa Afrika.

# Living
# One Law
# for One
# Nation

## 1997 - 2011

'You have to keep working at the Constitution. You can never give up. Democracies are generally noisy places in which there is much noise and contestation. It is oppressive and authoritarian societies that are silent. Our democracy is certainly wonderfully noisy and contested. We should neither be silenced by the noise nor deterred from pursuing the Constitution's vision by the contestation. It is important that all South Africans keep a clear head. Our Constitution's message is simple. We must acknowledge the injustices of the past that still mark our present and work to eradicate those injustices so that we can really free the potential of each South African.'

Justice Kate O'Regan

1

**1** Schoolchildren familiarising themselves
with the Constitution. © *Benny Gool /*
*Oryx Archives*

# A People's Constitution

## Overview

The Constitution of the Republic of South Africa, 1996, was certified by the Constitutional Court on 4 December 1996 and came into effect in February 1997. One of the last actions of the Constitutional Assembly was to distribute six million miniature-sized copies of the final text in all 11 languages free of charge to the people of South Africa. Cyril Ramaphosa expressed the hope of all members of the Constitutional Assembly that the legacy of their hard work did not merely reside in the pages of these books: *'The real legacy ... lies in the growing awareness of what a constitution means. I appeal to you all to nurture, to claim the Constitution as your own. We have a constitution we can be proud of, now let's make it work. It must become part of people's everyday lives.'*

The extent to which the Constitution has become part of people's lives is difficult to measure in any quantifiable way although a range of commentators all believe that it has had a profound impact on South African society. Hassen Ebrahim, who was in charge of the Constitutional Assembly's public participation campaign, believes that the template laid down by the Constitutional Assembly – namely that ordinary people have the capacity to influence the laws and workings of government – has had a major bearing over the last years: *'There has been a groundswell of interest amongst citizens in matters which were previously the exclusive preserve of government ... This is the fundamental ingredient required to ensure that the vision that the Constitution represents – becomes a reality.'*

According to Joyce Seroke, former head of the Commission for Gender Equality (CGE): *'That the Constitution has become part of people's everyday lives is evidenced by the recent protests calling out for quality of life – good housing, water, etc. People are articulating their concerns regarding corruption by high-ranking government officials and self-enrichment by some whilst the majority remains poor.'*

At a recent conference, FW de Klerk applauded the impressive track record of the media and civil society in defence of the Constitution. The examples he gave ranged from current actions in protesting against the Protection of Information Bill and proposals for a Media Appeals Tribunal to his applause for a single citizen, Hugh Glenister, in succeeding in having the government's abolition of the Scorpions, an agency that investigated and prosecuted organised crime and corruption, declared illegal in the Constitutional Court.

The independent state institutions set up in Chapter 9 of the Constitution – namely the Human Rights and Gender Commissions, the Public Protector and the Auditor-General, the Commission for the Promotion and Protection of the Rights of Cultural, Religious and Linguistic Communities, and the Independent Electoral Commission – are another key way in which the values of the Constitution have been nourished. These institutions were created with the express purpose of strengthening constitutional democracy in our country. They have faced considerable challenges over the years but have still had an important impact. Joyce Seroke explains: *'The Gender Commission has been plagued by insufficient funds and non-cooperation by some government departments. However, through its awareness-raising, it has created a platform for constructive debates on women's issues and women have begun to understand how they benefit from new legislation. It has represented women in the Constitutional Court, resulting in a number of Judgements that have affirmed women's rights.'*

Indeed, perhaps the most direct way of understanding the impact of the Constitution on individuals and communities is through the workings of the Constitutional Court – the prime upholder and enforcer of the Constitution. This chapter explains how the Court operates and investigates some of the key landmark cases that have had an important bearing on our constitutional democracy.

# The Constitutional Court

After a long process to choose a location for the new building, the Constitutional Court settled on the site of the city's notorious Old Fort prison where human rights had been flouted for nearly a century. The spectacular new court building was opened on 21 March, Human Rights Day, in 2004. At the moving ceremony, President Thabo Mbeki described the building as an 'architectural jewel' and believed that the Court's location made 'the categorical statement that our country has broken with its past of despotic and tyrannical misrule'. He proclaimed the Court 'a shining beacon of hope for the protection of human rights and the advancement of human liberty and dignity'.

Hundreds of dignitaries including 37 judges from around the world, South Africa's own legal community, several Cabinet ministers and members of the Constitutional Assembly watched 27 children, all born in 1994, come up to the podium to recite the rights enshrined in the Constitution in the 11 official languages. The President then declared the seat of the highest court in the land open. The great wooden doors to the court, engraved with the 27 fundamental constitutional rights, swung open to admit President Mbeki, his wife Zanele, Chief Justice Arthur Chaskalson, the Constitutional Court Justices, Speaker of Parliament Frene Ginwala, Deputy Minister of Justice Cheryl Gillwald, Johannesburg mayor Amos Masondo (once a political prisoner at the Old Fort) and Sam Shilowa. In this acclaimed new building, the 11 judges stand guard over the Constitution.

Since its first sitting in the death penalty case in February 1995, the Constitutional Court has received an increasing number of applications each year – from 26 in 1994 to 118 in 2010. It has also set down an increasing number of cases for oral argument. In 1995, the Court handed down 14 judgements in such cases; in 2010 the number was 24. This steady increase undoubtedly indicates civil society's growing awareness of constitutional rights in South Africa, an increased activism in bringing cases to the Court, and the entrenchment of the Court as an institution in our democracy. General media coverage has confirmed

this. According to the law clerks Claire Avidon and Lwando Xaso, *'The Court's significant number of applications each year is an indication that South Africans are engaging more with the judiciary. The Constitution is a living document and its interpretation is a mirror of this country's ongoing dialogue. We have had definite victories and definite losses, but fortunately we are still committed to the constitutional project.'*

**1** The engraved doors of the Constitutional Court. © *David Klemanski*

**2** A night view of the new Constitutional Court building. © *Angela Buckland*

1

# The hearings

The Court deals mostly with applications to appeal against judgements of other courts. But on rare occasions it can also deal with matters directly. Litigants file their applications with the Registrar. A copy is given to each of the 11 justices, who directly apply themselves to and engage with the issues in the application. The procedures in each justice's chamber vary. In some chambers, a memo (with a recommendation as to whether the case should be heard or not) is prepared by one of the law clerks and is circulated to the rest of the chamber for discussion.

The justices usually meet weekly in conference to debate the new applications. While the law clerks provide invaluable research, all decisions relating to the disposition of any dispute before the Court remain the sole duty and responsibility of the judge concerned. Sometimes, the debates are continued after conference, between individual justices by email

or in person or between all the judges. The justices then decide whether the case will be set down for hearing or dismissed.

All the justices usually hear matters before the Court. A quorum of at least eight judges is required. Parties present written arguments prior to the hearings. The actual hearings provide an opportunity for debate around the more difficult issues raised by these written arguments. Organisations that have expert knowledge of the subjects under discussion are permitted to address argument to the Court as *amicus curiae*, or friend of the Court.

When the justices have heard all the arguments they retire to discuss the case and vote on which position they support. The Chief Justice appoints one member to write the majority opinion, which is circulated for comment. The justices who agree with the majority

1

judgement sign the document. They are free to write their own judgement if they wish to express different reasons for concurring. Equally, those who are opposed to the majority decision are free to write their own dissenting judgement. The Court has handed down a number of judgements that have had a profound impact on the law in South Africa.

Early landmark judgements set a precedent for the many cases that have been presented to the Court in the 16 years of its existence. The right to dignity, in keeping with the African philosophy of *ubuntu*, was fundamental to the Court's first case in which the death penalty was declared unconstitutional, and has been a guiding principle in the hearings that have followed. In the death penalty judgement, President Arthur Chaskalson found:

*'The rights to life and dignity are the most important of all human rights, and the source of all other personal rights in Chapter 3. By committing ourselves to a society founded on the recognition of human rights we are required to value these two rights above all others. And this must be demonstrated by the State in everything that it does, including the way it punishes criminals.'*

**1** The Constitutional Court in session. © *Guto Bussab*

# The landmark cases (1996-2011)

## The right to vote
*August and Another v Electoral
Commission and Others* (1999)

In 1998 two prisoners, Arnold August and Veronica Mabutho wrote to the Independent Electoral Commission (IEC) seeking an undertaking that they and all other prisoners would be allowed to vote in the April 1999 general election. Having not received a reply for four months, they sought a court order declaring that all prisoners should be allowed to vote in the election. The High Court dismissed the application, saying that the special logistical and administrative measures required to accommodate prisoners should be reserved for those voters 'whose predicament was not of their own making'. The IEC was absolved of any obligation to ensure that prisoners could vote, which in effect disbarred prisoners from voting. Relying on the right to vote, the right to equality and the right to dignity, Mr August and Ms Mabutho sought leave to appeal to the Constitutional Court.

The Constitutional Court had to decide whether to issue an order that all prisoners were entitled to register as voters on the national voters' roll and to vote in the general elections. Counsel for the prisoners contended that the political rights of all South African citizens are entrenched in Section 1(d) of the Constitution. And while the 1998 Amendment to the Electoral Act lists certain conditions that preclude people from registering to vote, it does not exclude all prisoners from the voters' roll but only those convicted of exceptionally violent crimes without the option of a fine. It is the duty of the IEC to make provisions for all other prisoners to vote.

Mr August and Ms Mabutho's position was supported by the Centre for Applied Legal Studies, which presented the Court with statistics to show that a high number of prisoners were being held in jail because they were simply too poor to pay even the minimum bail or fine. Not allowing them to vote would be unfair and discriminatory.

Counsel for the Electoral Commission and the Correctional Services claimed that while the Department of Correctional Services, unlike the IEC, had not opposed the prisoners' application to vote, it was not their responsibility to arrange for prisoners to vote. The meaning of the provision in the Electoral Act that someone is not allowed to vote if 'they are not ordinarily resident in the voting district for which that person has applied for registration' was questioned by the IEC in its effort to assess the logistical implications of prisoners voting.

In a unanimous judgement, the Constitutional Court declared that denying any citizen the right to vote was in breach of Section 19 of the Constitution and undermined South Africa's character as a democracy. Since prisoners are forced to 'eat, sleep and exercise in prison', they would be 'ordinarily resident' in prison and would be entitled to receive a special vote there, just as any citizen with a disability would be entitled to vote in his or her home. The Court ruled that all persons, other than certain categories of convicted prisoners, were entitled to vote. It was the duty of the IEC to make all reasonable arrangements for prisoners to do so.

Later, Parliament passed legislation seeking to prohibit voting by all prisoners serving a sentence of imprisonment without the options of a fine. The validity of this provision was challenged by the National Institution for Crime Prevention (NICRO) in a case that also went to the Constitutional Court. The Court held that the legislation had been badly drafted, and that adequate reasons for disenfranchising all prisoners in this category had not been advanced. The provision was therefore held to be inconsistent with the Constitution and invalid.

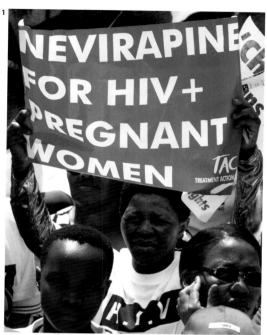

Section 27 of the Constitution provides:

1. Everyone has the right to have access to healthcare services, including reproductive healthcare.

2. The state must take reasonable legislative and other measures, within its available resources, to achieve the progressive realisation of these rights.

**1** Women protesting against the limited access to Nevirapine.
© *The Bigger Picture / Reuters*

## Significance

This was a landmark case in that the Constitution afforded the most vulnerable people in our society the power to effect positive change in their lives. In June 2009, Health Minister Dr Aaron Motsoaledi reported that mother-to-child infections had been reduced by as much as 96 per cent.

# Criminal procedure and the judiciary

*Alix Jean Carmichele v The Minister of Safety and Security and
the Minister of Justice and Constitutional Development* (2001)

In August 1995, Alix Carmichele came upon François Coetzee who had illegally entered her friend Julie Gosling's home in the small seaside town of Noetzie. Coetzee, who had been released on bail pending a case of raping a teenage girl, overpowered Carmichele and savagely attacked her, causing her serious permanent damage. Coetzee was arrested and charged with housebreaking and attempted murder and was sentenced to an effective twelve and a half years' imprisonment.

Ms Carmichele sued the government for damages, claiming that the police and public prosecutors had been negligent in their legal duty in not taking steps to prevent Coetzee, who had a history of violent crimes of a sexual nature, from harming her. It transpired that when Coetzee appeared in court on the initial charge of rape, the prosecutor failed to provide the magistrate with any information about Coetzee's history or previous convictions and the investigating police officer had indicated that Coetzee could be released on warning. Before Coetzee was due to appear in court again, he attempted suicide – as his mother had feared – and was taken to hospital for treatment. On his release the senior prosecutor in Knysna referred Coetzee for psychiatric observation. At the end of 30 days, the medical authorities deemed him fit to stand trial. Coetzee pleaded not guilty in the trial court and the case was postponed. Members of the community, including Gosling, who had found Coetzee snooping around her house on a number of occasions, approached the police, saying that they were afraid that he might strike again, but the police did nothing. It was during this time that Coetzee attacked Carmichele.

The Supreme Court of Appeal, using pre-constitutional law, found that the police could only be held liable for acts they had committed, not for what they had failed to do – in this case, to protect Ms Carmichele from Coetzee. In 2001 Carmichele took the case to the Constitutional Court.

The Constitutional Court was asked to decide whether the investigating police officer and the prosecutor should have opposed the granting of bail and brought Coetzee's background to the attention of the magistrate instead of informing the magistrate that Coetzee could be released on warning, and later allowing that to stand after he was released from hospital.

Counsel for Ms Carmichele submitted that the Court of Appeal had erred in applying pre-constitutional law since the Constitution expressly states that the courts are obliged to develop pre-constitutional common law to bring it in line with the values of the Constitution. The Constitution provides citizens with the rights to life, equality, dignity, freedom and security and, for the first time, makes the state responsible to the public for protecting these rights.

The Court concluded that 'although the major engine for law reform should be the legislature, Courts are under a general duty to develop the common law when it deviates from the spirit, purport and objects of the Bill of Rights'.

The Court held that the Constitution placed positive obligations on the state, including an obligation to protect women, and that the trial court should have considered whether, as a result of these obligations, the common law should have been developed to protect Ms Carmichele. It referred the matter back to the trial court to hear relevant evidence on this issue. The trial court upheld Ms Carmichele's claim and this decision was affirmed on appeal to the Supreme Court of Appeal.

Sections 9, 10, 11, 12 and 13 of the Constitution provide for the rights to equality, dignity, life, freedom and security of the person and privacy.

Section 39(2) states, 'When interpreting any legislation, and when developing the common law or customary law, every court, tribunal or forum must promote the spirit, purport and objects of the Bill of Rights.'

## Significance

*Carmichele* is a leading case on the duty of courts to develop the common law where appropriate and to bring it into conformity with the spirit of the Bill of Rights. The case made real the state's duty to protect the public in general, but more particularly to protect the dignity, freedom and security of women. This case was hailed as a victory for women in South Africa. Twelve years after her attack, Ms Carmichele was compensated for the damages she had suffered.

*'Few things can be more important to women than freedom from the threat of sexual violence ... Sexual violence and the threat of sexual violence goes to the core of women's subordination in society. It is the single greatest threat to the self-determination of South African women.'*
- Justices Laurie Ackermann and Richard Goldstone in a joint judgement

# The right to land

*Alexkor Ltd and Another v Richtersveld
Community and Others* (2003)

The Richtersveld case began in 1988 when a small rural community in the Richtersveld claimed indigenous title to 84 000 hectares of land in the Land Claims Court (LCC) under the Restitution of Land Rights Act of 1994. The land had been annexed by the Cape in 1847. In 1925 it was given to Alexkor, a government-owned mining company, after diamonds were discovered in the area. Ten years of complex litigation ensued around the indigenous title claim, with the matter going backwards and forwards between the High Court, the LCC, the Supreme Court of Appeal (SCA), and the Constitutional Court.

The LCC dismissed the community's claim, holding that the dispossession had occurred at the time of annexation in 1847. The Land Restitution Act specified that in order for there to be restitution, dispossession had to have happened after the Natives Land Act was adopted on 19 June 1913 and be the result of racial discrimination. In 2003 the claim was upheld on appeal by the SCA, which found that the community had in fact been in possession of the whole of the Richtersveld prior to and after 1847. Their rights had been ignored when diamonds were discovered in the area and when the government granted full ownership of the land to Alexkor. The SCA ordered that the Richtersveld community was entitled to restitution. Alexkor sought special leave to appeal to the Constitutional Court.

The Constitutional Court deliberated on the many complex issues that had been raised in the earlier judgement. What was particularly groundbreaking was the application of indigenous law to determine one of the key issues of the case: whether the community had in fact held indigenous title to the land in the 1920s and, if so, whether this indigenous title extended to its natural resources, particularly its precious stones.

In order to meet the Constitution's injunction that all courts apply indigenous law where applicable, the Court said, 'The content of the land rights held by the community must be determined by reference to the history and the usages of the community of

Richtersveld.' Witnesses on behalf of the community provided oral testimony to support their claims to indigenous title and asserted that the local Nama had mined for minerals prior to British annexation and had in fact granted mineral leases to outsiders until 1910. Counsel for Alexkor held that even if the community had extracted minerals, this became unlawful after 1847 when the area became property of the British Crown. The Court found nothing in the annexation proclamation to suggest that the annexation of the area had extinguished the land rights of the community.

Evidence presented to the Court indicated that the indigenous ownership of the Richtersveld community remained intact when the Land Act was passed and continued until the mid-1920s when diamonds were found. At this point the community was effectively dispossessed of its land. While white people whose land rights had been registered in the Deeds Office were protected by the Precious Stones Act of 1927, indigenous title owners of the land who were not registered were deprived of almost all their property rights. The Court upheld that the failure to recognise indigenous law ownership was based on racial discrimination.

As Justice Yacoob stated, 'If you were white your claim was taken seriously. If you were there a hundred years it was taken very seriously, but if you were black you were nothing.'

The Court found that the Richtersveld community held ownership of the land under indigenous law and was entitled 'to restitution of the ownership of the subject land (including its minerals and precious stones) and to the exclusive beneficial use and occupation thereof'. The Court ordered the matter to be referred back to the Land Claims Court for the determination of the nature of the restitution.

Section 211(3) of the Constitution provides:

The courts must apply customary law when that law is applicable, subject to the Constitution and any legislation that specifically deals with customary law.

1 People of the Richtersveld.
© Paul Weinberg / Africa
Media Online

## Significance

In 2007 the Richtersveld community won its 10-year case and secured a 49 per cent stake in Alexkor, plus large tracts of land and more than R200 million in compensation. The case also set a precedent for indigenous law to be regarded as an integral part of our law.

'This is a big moment in the history of the Richtersveld and South Africa. To wait 80 years for your land is not easy.' - Willem Diergaardt, community leader

# Equality

*Minister of Home Affairs and Another v Fourie and Another;*
*Lesbian and Gay Equality Project and Others v Minister* (2005)

The case was unusual in that two separate cases pertaining to the same issues were heard in the Constitutional Court on the same day.

The applicants in the first case, Adriaana Fourie and Cecelia Johanna Bonthuys, who had been living together as a couple for 10 years, wanted to get married. Their case was heard in the High Court and the Supreme Court of Appeal, but it was made clear that since they had not in fact challenged the Marriage Act, in which marriage is explicitly defined as being between a man and a woman, their proposed marriage would be unlawful. The Supreme Court of Appeal upheld their right to marry and ruled that the common-law definition of marriage should be developed to embrace same-sex couples. However, the Court said that any amendment to the actual Marriage Act was a matter for Parliament.

In the second case the Lesbian and Gay Equality Project (the Equality Project), argued that the common law definition of marriage and the Marriage Act were unconstitutional in that they violated the rights to equality, dignity and privacy.

In the Constitutional Court two broad issues were addressed. The Court had to decide whether the fact that no provision was made for same-sex couples to marry each other was unconstitutional in terms of Section 9(3) and, if so, what the appropriate remedy for the unconstitutionality should be.

Counsel for the Minister of Justice argued that although the Constitution defended the rights of same-sex couples, it did not explicitly protect the right to marry. The Court held that although the Bill of Rights does not expressly include a right to marry, 'it does not follow that the Constitution does nothing to protect that right and, with it, the right to be treated equally and with dignity in the exercise of that right'.

Members of religious organisations argued against the reform of South Africa's marriage laws, citing passages from the Bible to claim that marriage is an inherently procreative relationship between a man and a woman and asserting that the legalisation of same-sex marriages would infringe on the rights of many South Africans to religious freedom. While the Court was respectful of the role religion plays in the lives of South Africans, it held that religious doctrine could not be used in interpreting the Constitution.

In delivering the judgement of the majority of the Court, Justice Sachs said the exclusion of same-sex couples from marriage was unfairly discriminatory, unconstitutional and invalid. *'It reinforces the wounding notion that they are to be treated as biological oddities, as failed or lapsed human beings who do not fit into normal society, and, as such, do not qualify for the full moral concern and respect that our Constitution seeks to secure for everyone. It signifies that their capacity for love, commitment and accepting responsibility is by definition less worthy of regard than that of heterosexual couples.'*

The Court ordered that same-sex couples be enabled to enjoy the status, benefits and responsibilities that marriage offers to heterosexual couples and that the wording of the Marriage Act be amended accordingly. The Court suspended the order for one year to allow Parliament to debate the issue and decide how it would legalise same-sex marriage. One day before the Court's deadline, Parliament enacted the Civil Union Act of 2006. It accommodated the religious community in that it left the Marriage Act intact but made it possible for same-sex couples to legally marry under the new Civil Union Act.

Section 9(3) of the Constitution provides:

The state may not unfairly discriminate directly or indirectly against anyone on one or more grounds, including race, gender, sex, pregnancy, marital status, ethnic or social origin, colour, sexual orientation, age, disability, religion, conscience, belief, culture, language and birth.

1

**1** Charles Januarie and Hompie Ndimande after their civil union marriage. © Zanele Maholi

## Significance

The judgement made evident that the Constitutional Court is unwavering in its enforcement of the rights to equality and protection against unfair discrimination. The Civil Union Act has transformed the lives of same-sex couples, who can now choose to marry and have the same legal recognition and benefits as heterosexual couples. Today, South Africa is one of only 10 countries in the world that grant full legal recognition to same-sex marriages.

*'Our people must have the assurance that there will be protection when they choose to depart from the majoritarian norm, provided the purpose served is legitimate. We should have a society that is capable of enduring that, living with that, and making sure that indeed it becomes a proud part of all of us.'*
– Deputy Chief Justice Moseneke

# Equality
*Hoffman v South African Airways* (2000)

Jacques Hoffman was one of 20 candidates chosen for the position of cabin attendant with South African Airways (SAA), subject to a medical examination. Although Mr Hoffman was found to be suitably fit, an HIV/Aids blood test showed that he was HIV-positive. According to SAA policy, this rendered him 'unsuitable' and he was refused employment. Having unsuccessfully challenged the constitutionality of the policy in the High Court, Mr Hoffman applied directly to the Constitutional Court for an order forcing SAA to employ him.

The Court had to decide whether SAA had violated Mr Hoffman's constitutional right to equality, dignity and fair labour practices. According to SAA, cabin attendants are required to fly to countries where yellow fever is endemic; those living with HIV might not be able to tolerate the yellow fever vaccination, and might therefore contract and transmit the disease to passengers. They were also prone to opportunistic disease which if contracted could be passed on to passengers. In addition, SAA held that because of their limited life expectancy people who are HIV-positive do not warrant the costs of training. SAA's own medical expert in fact presented evidence that illustrated that SAA's assertions were not true of all persons who are HIV-positive and were not true of Jacques Hoffman.

The Court found: 'The fact that some people who are HIV-positive may, under certain circumstances, be unsuitable for employment as cabin attendants does not justify the exclusion from employment as cabin attendants of all people who are living with HIV.' Furthermore, the judges were unanimous in their opinion that denying Mr Hoffman employment because he was living with HIV constituted unfair discrimination and impaired his dignity. SAA was ordered to offer to employ Mr Hoffman as a cabin attendant.

Section 9 of the Constitution provides:

(1) Everyone is equal before the law and has the right to equal protection and benefit of the law.

(3) The state may not unfairly discriminate directly or indirectly against anyone on one or more grounds, including race, gender, sex, pregnancy, marital status, ethnic or social origin, colour, sexual orientation, age, disability, religion, conscience, belief, culture, language and birth ...

(5) Discrimination on one or more of the grounds listed in subsection (3) is unfair unless it is established that the discrimination is fair.

## Significance

This was a landmark case for the many South Africans who are living with HIV or Aids. The Court held that the constitutional right not to be unfairly discriminated against, 'cannot be determined by ill-informed public perception of persons with HIV'.

*'The impact of discrimination on HIV-positive people is devastating. It is even more so when it occurs in the context of employment. It denies them the right to earn a living. For this reason they enjoy special protection in our law.'* – Justice Ngcobo

# The impact of the landmark cases

These and other 'landmark' cases have had a wide-ranging impact on issues such as socio-economic rights, public power and criminal procedure. According to former Chief Justice Arthur Chaskalson, 'In the course of 16 years, the Court has established itself as the apex court of the judiciary with an international reputation. Its decisions have helped to shape a new jurisprudence consistent with the values of our Constitution, and to give substance to the commitments made in the Bill of Rights. It is, and is perceived to be, one of the pillars of our democracy.'

For law clerks Lwando Xaso and Claire Avidon, the highlight of their work at the Court has been 'experiencing how a judgement handed down by this Court can single-handedly rectify a grave injustice and restore society's faith in the legal process. Sitting in the Court, observing the community members that have come to hear their story put before this Court for adjudication ... has changed our understanding of the Constitution. At law school, where the privileged few pursue legal education, the Constitution may seem an elite document or a lawyer's tool that is far removed from everyday realities as academics pour over its abstract meanings. This is not the case.'

1 The Richtersveld. © Adam Broomberg & Oliver Chanarin

Deputy Chief Justice Dikgang Moseneke, who has been a member of the Constitutional Court for nearly a decade, believes that the Court 'has fearlessly pronounced on vital disputes and in so doing has produced a jurisprudence that we can be proud of'. In particular, he believes that 'the equality jurisprudence of our Court is a matter of great pride and is world-renowned. It has unhesitatingly banished discrimination and exclusion on every conceivable ground.'

Indeed, the Court's judgements have sparked off much interest in legal communities around the world. Professors, academics and former drafters of the Constitution have attended various gatherings to scrutinise the cases that have been heard and all agree that the Constitutional Court has developed 'path-breaking and innovative human rights jurisprudence' that has underpinned the Constitution's transformative goals. In a tenth anniversary publication of the Constitutional Court, Iain Currie, Victoria Bronstein and Marius Pieterse wrote: 'The Court has become a respected feature of the South African political landscape. Its jurisprudence has had an extraordinarily invigorating effect on the South African legal system, waking it from the demoralising slumbers in which it had languished for the best part of a century. These are considerable achievements worthy of celebration.'

For the writers of the Constitution, the Court's rulings are the real manifestation of its status as a living document. Cyril Ramaphosa says that he 'gets goosebumps' when reading the decisions that have been made. 'It gives life to our Constitution. It confirms that our Constitution is not just some sterile document. It has life, it has legs, it has eyes, it has arms to wrap itself around the people of South Africa. This is how the Constitution is alive.'

# Not without difficulties

However, the high praise for the work of the Court does not mean that it – or the Constitution itself – has been without difficulties. Interestingly, many of the controversies that have erupted in recent times hark back to the very considerations that nearly scuppered the negotiation process during the time of the writing of the interim and final constitutions.

An issue, for example, that began at Kempton Park and has continued to be a focus of debate relates to the composition of the Court and the judicial appointments made by the Judicial Service Commission (JSC). Many have questioned the extent of the progress that has been made in remedying the skewed race and gender balance of the judiciary in South Africa relative to the pre-1994 situation. Commenting on the issue of the demographics of the bench, Justice O'Regan believes that the Constitutional Court has been more successfully transformed in racial rather than gender terms:

'Throughout our 15 years at the Court, Justice Mokgoro and I both felt that it was important that we performed our jobs as well as we could so that we would open rather than close doors for future female judges. However, few female judges have been appointed to the Court. There are still only two women on the Court, the same number as in 1994. By contrast, in 1994 there were seven white judges and four black judges. There are now eight black judges and three white judges. The rate of transformation on race has far outstripped transformation on gender.'

This slow pace of gender transformation of the judiciary came into the spotlight in October 2009 when vacancies opened on the Court at the time of the retirement of Justices O'Regan, Mokgoro and Sachs. The legal community hoped that the JSC would take corrective action and appoint more women judges to the Court. These hopes were dashed when three men – Chris Jafta, Johan Froneman and Mogoeng Mogoeng – and only one woman – Sisi Khampepe –

were ultimately appointed. At a conference in late 2010, former Justice Mokgoro spoke out frankly on this issue and the judiciary more broadly. She said that while South Africa has started to break ground on the appointments of women judges and has its first woman Judge President,

'… the picture remains wholly unsatisfactory despite the passage of time. In a society such as ours, where patriarchy is so deeply entrenched, affecting adversely the everyday lives of so many women … the need for women both in the judiciary as a whole and in leadership positions in particular cannot be exaggerated. Although we have come a long way, we must agree that we have just scratched the surface. We must step up our efforts … the position of women on the Bench has become rather desperate. That calls for our measures and approaches to become much more creative.'

Over the last years, there have been several more serious controversies around judicial transformation as well as the independence of the judiciary. In 2008, one such controversy exploded when the justices of the Constitutional Court issued a statement reporting that they had referred the Cape Judge President, Judge Hlophe, to the JSC because they maintained that Hlophe had made 'an improper attempt to influence this Court's pending judgement in one or more cases'. It was subsequently reported that Hlophe was alleged by unnamed sources to have approached Justices Nkabinde and Jafta separately in their offices and told them that he would be next Chief Justice and that they should consider their future and rule in favour of Zuma in a case that was before the Constitutional Court. Judge Hlophe vehemently denied the charge. A flurry of accusations and counter accusations and court applications ensued. At the time of writing, the matter has still not been resolved and is the subject of consideration by the JSC.

On the eve of the fifteenth anniversary of the Constitution, the Court has faced perhaps its greatest challenge, again relating to the issue of judicial appointments. This time, the issue focused on the appointment of a new Chief Justice. The controversy first exploded in the media in July 2011, when President Jacob Zuma attempted to extend the term of the sitting Chief Justice, Sandile Ngcobo. There was an outcry against this, not because of Ngcobo's credentials, which were considered impeccable, but because it was deemed unconstitutional. Indeed the Constitutional Court itself ultimately ruled the process was against the provisions of the Constitution. They found that the extension 'violated the principle of judicial independence' stating that 'this kind of open-ended discretion may raise a reasonable apprehension or perception that the independence of the Chief Justice, and, by corollary, the judiciary, may be undermined by external interference of the Executive. The truth may be different, but it matters not. What matters is that the judiciary must be seen to be free from external interference.'

This was followed by further controversy over President Zuma's nomination of Justice Mogoeng Mogoeng as the next Chief Justice. Concerns were raised in many quarters about Mogoeng's relative lack of experience and the content of some of his previous judgements. Mogoeng's televised interview with the JSC was long and gruelling, with many tense exchanges. President Zuma said of the process afterwards: 'The interview was no doubt the longest, most transparent and most robust ever undertaken by a candidate of Chief Justice in the history of this young democracy.' Ultimately, the JSC confirmed Mogoeng's appointment as Chief Justice.

Other commentators have questioned the legitimacy of the Constitution itself. Deputy Chief Justice Moseneke, speaking at a public lecture at the University of Cape Town in October 2011, summarised the position that has emerged against the constitutional arrangement:

'The argument starts from the premise that the Constitution is an awful bargain shaped by inapt concessions during the negotiations in 1993. The compromise, the argument goes, is characterised by two primary blemishes. First, the will of the people does not find full voice within constitutional arrangements. For that reason the legislative and executive power in the hands of the parliamentary majority is empty. Second, the constitutional constraints on the exercise of public power stand in the way of government to deliver on social equity. That is another way of saying that the Constitution has shielded the historic economic inequality, and obstructs the effective economic participation or freedom of the majority.'

The Deputy Chief Justice's address went on to counter these accusations. In relation to the issue of weakened state authority, Moseneke said: 'A claim that constitutionalism amounts only to limiting government is misleading and potentially dangerous. A robust and supreme constitution arguably can make government stronger and more stable. Institutional arrangements such as the separation of powers, checks and balances, and individual civil, political and justiciable socio-economic rights make the government more responsible, more consistent, more predictable, more just, more caring, more responsive and more legitimate in the eyes of the citizenry.'

The debates around judicial appointments, the independence of the judiciary and the constitution lie at the heart of a healthy democratic society. The kind of dialogue and debate taking place at the moment will no doubt continue for years to come. Those who sat around the table to forge South Africa's democracy, first at Kempton Park and then in the Constitutional Assembly, remain optimistic about the Constitution. Fifteen years on, they still regard it as the most important foundation for confronting South Africa's many challenges. Speaking at a recent conference, FW de Klerk concluded his address on how to ensure long-term sustainable development in South Africa by emphasising the importance of the Constitution and harking back to the negotiation period: *'I believe that the degree to which we abide by our Constitution will be a critical factor in ensuring sustainable development for our country. It is, after all, the foundation of our society … It defines and protects a vast array of rights for all South Africans. All South Africans should work together to achieve the vision set out in the Constitution … We need to talk with one another in the frank and constructive way that we did during the negotiations of the 1990s.'*

In his sequel to *Long Walk to Freedom*, Nelson Mandela comes to a similar conclusion when reflecting on the political challenges faced by this country in the era of democracy: *'All these considerations, as important as they may be, should never be allowed to undermine our democratic Constitution, which guarantees unqualified citizenship rights to all South Africans … It has a Bill of Rights on which a citizen can rely if any of his or her rights are threatened or violated. All of us, without exception, are called upon to respect that Constitution.'*

Cyril Ramaphosa is equally clear that the Constitution is the basis for fortifying South Africa's democratic future: *'Democracy was never going to be a bed of roses. It is a process that unfolds on an ongoing basis. There will be high moments and low moments. As ordinary people we may even sometimes doubt whether this Constitution is helping us achieve what we always dreamt of. There will be times when even the judiciary will be put under enormous tests and strain in upholding the Constitution. But even if our rulers can go mad and lose their heads we have got this Constitution. Even if someone stands on the podium and says something against the Bill of Rights, we know that it will not erode our rights. It simply cannot happen. And for me that is my Rock of Gibraltar. It is the rock of my constitutional soul. I hold on to it. There is nothing that gives me more confidence, more hope, and more security and a sense of stability than this Constitution.'*

It is the young law clerks Lwando Xaso and Claire Avidon, who work at the Court today and who are the future potential leaders of tomorrow, who perhaps best capture the spirit of the Constitution in broadening and securing our democracy: *'The Constitution is our inheritance. Its existence requires our utmost respect in that it was hard won following a fierce struggle that should not be forgotten. Despite the respect that it requires, this does not mean that it is not to be challenged or engaged with. The Constitution is a dynamic document and its boundaries are there to be tested. As its custodian, society needs to take responsibility and ownership of it and vigilantly guard against its subversion. As young people we need to facilitate debates and challenges about the Constitution to ensure it continues to unite us in our diversity.'*

# Bill of Rights

Mandela

## Rights

7. (1) This Bill of Rights is a cornerstone of democracy in South Africa. It enshrines the rights of all people in our country and affirms the democratic values of human dignity, equality and freedom.
(2) The state must respect, protect, promote and fulfil the rights in the Bill of Rights.
(3) The rights in the Bill of Rights are subject to the limitations contained or referred to in section 36, or elsewhere in the Bill.

## Application

8. (1) The Bill of Rights applies to all law, and binds the legislature, the executive, the judiciary and all organs of state.
(2) A provision of the Bill of Rights binds a natural or a juristic person if, and to the extent that, it is applicable, taking into account the nature of the right and the nature of any duty imposed by the right.
(3) When applying a provision of the Bill of Rights to a natural or juristic person in terms of subsection (2), a court –
(a) in order to give effect to a right in the Bill, must apply, or if necessary develop, the common law to the extent that legislation does not give effect to that right; and
(b) may develop rules of the common law to limit the right, provided that the limitation is in accordance with section 36 (1).
(4) A juristic person is entitled to the rights in the Bill of Rights to the extent required by the nature of the rights and the nature of that juristic person.

## Equality

9. (1) Everyone is equal before the law and has the right to equal protection and benefit of the law.
(2) Equality includes the full and equal enjoyment of all rights and freedoms. To promote the achievement of equality, legislative and other measures designed to protect or advance persons, or categories of persons, disadvantaged by unfair discrimination may be taken.
(3) The state may not unfairly discriminate directly or indirectly against anyone on one or more grounds, including race, gender, sex, pregnancy, marital status, ethnic or social origin, colour, sexual orientation, age, disability, religion, conscience, belief, culture, language and birth.
(4) No person may unfairly discriminate directly or indirectly against anyone on one or more grounds in terms of subsection (3). National legislation must be enacted to prevent or prohibit unfair discrimination.
(5) Discrimination on one or more of the grounds listed in subsection (3) is unfair unless it is established that the discrimination is fair.

## Human dignity

10. Everyone has inherent dignity and the right to have their dignity respected and protected.

## Life

11. Everyone has the right to life.

## Freedom and security of the person.

12. (1) Everyone has the right to freedom and security of the person, which includes the right –
(a) not to be deprived of freedom arbitrarily or without just cause;
(b) not to be detained without trial;
(c) to be free from all forms of violence from either public or private sources;
(d) not to be tortured in any way; and
(e) not to be treated or punished in a cruel, inhuman or degrading way.
(2) Everyone has the right to bodily and psychological integrity, which includes the right –
(a) to make decisions concerning reproduction;
(b) to security in and control over their body; and
(c) not to be subjected to medical or scientific experiments without their informed consent.

## Slavery, servitude and forced labour

13. No one may be subjected to slavery, servitude or forced labour.

## Privacy

14. Everyone has the right to privacy, which includes the right not to have –
(a) their person or home searched;
(b) their property searched;
(c) their possessions seized; or
(d) the privacy of their communications infringed.

## Freedom of religion, belief and opinion

15. (1) Everyone has the right to freedom of conscience, religion, thought, belief and opinion.
(2) Religious observances may be conducted at state or state-aided institutions, provided that –
(a) those observances follow rules made by the appropriate public authorities;
(b) they are conducted on an equitable basis; and
(c) attendance at them is free and voluntary.
(3) (a) This section does not prevent legislation recognising –
(i) marriages concluded under any tradition, or a system of religious, personal or family law; or
(ii) systems of personal and family law under any tradition, or adhered to by persons professing a particular religion.
(b) Recognition in terms of paragraph (a) must be consistent with this section and the other provisions of the Constitution.

## Freedom of expression

16. (1) Everyone has the right to freedom of expression, which includes –
(a) freedom of the press and other media;
(b) freedom to receive or impart information or ideas;
(c) freedom of artistic creativity; and
(d) academic freedom and freedom of scientific research.
(2) The right in subsection (1) does not extend to –
(a) propaganda for war;
(b) incitement of imminent violence; or
(c) advocacy of hatred that is based on race, ethnicity, gender or religion, and that constitutes incitement to cause harm.

## Assembly, demonstration, picket and petition

17. Everyone has the right, peacefully and unarmed, to assemble, to demonstrate, to picket and to present petitions.

## Freedom of association

18. Everyone has the right to freedom of association.

## Political rights

19. (1) Every citizen is free to make political choices, which includes the right –
(a) to form a political party;
(b) to participate in the activities of, or recruit members for, a political party; and
(c) to campaign for a political party or cause.
(2) Every citizen has the right to free, fair and regular elections for any legislative body established in terms of the Constitution.
(3) Every adult citizen has the right –
(a) to vote in elections for any legislative body established in terms of the Constitution, and to do so in secret; and
(b) to stand for public office and, if elected, to hold office.

## Citizenship

20. No citizen may be deprived of citizenship.

## Freedom of movement and residence

21. (1) Everyone has the right to freedom of movement.
(2) Everyone has the right to leave the Republic.
(3) Every citizen has the right to enter, to remain in and to reside anywhere in the Republic.
(4) Every citizen has the right to a passport.

## Freedom of trade, occupation and profession

22. Every citizen has the right to choose their trade, occupation or profession freely. The practice of a trade, occupation or profession may be regulated by law.

## Labour relations

23. (1) Everyone has the right to fair labour practices.
(2) Every worker has the right –
(a) to form and join a trade union;
(b) to participate in the activities and programmes of a trade union; and
(c) to strike.
(3) Every employer has the right –
(a) to form and join an employers' organisation; and
(b) to participate in the activities and programmes of an employers' organisation.
(4) Every trade union and every employers' organisation has the right –
(a) to determine its own administration, programmes and activities;
(b) to organise; and
(c) to form and join a federation.
(5) Every trade union, employers' organisation and employer has the right to engage in collective bargaining. National legislation may be enacted to regulate collective bargaining. To the extent that the legislation may limit a right in this Chapter, the limitation must comply with section 36 (1).
(6) National legislation may recognise union security arrangements contained in collective agreements. To the extent that the legislation may limit a right in this Chapter, the limitation must comply with section 36 (1).

## Environment

24. Everyone has the right –
(a) to an environment that is not harmful to their health or well-being; and
(b) to have the environment protected, for the benefit of present and future generations, through reasonable legislative and other measures that –
(i) prevent pollution and ecological degradation;
(ii) promote conservation; and
(iii) secure ecologically sustainable development and use of natural resources while promoting justifiable economic and social development.

## Property

25. (1) No one may be deprived of property except in terms of law of general application, and no law may permit arbitrary deprivation of property.
(2) Property may be expropriated only in terms of law of general application –
(a) for a public purpose or in the public interest; and
(b) subject to compensation, the amount of which and the time and manner of payment of which have either been agreed to by those affected or decided or approved by a court.
(3) The amount of the compensation and the time and manner of payment must be just and equitable, reflecting an equitable balance between the public interest and the interests of those affected, having regard to all relevant circumstances, including-
(a) the current use of the property;
(b) the history of the acquisition and use of the property;
(c) the market value of the property;
(d) the extent of direct state investment and subsidy in the acquisition and beneficial capital improvement of the property; and
(e) the purpose of the expropriation.
(4) For the purposes of this section –
(a) the public interest includes the nation's commitment to land reform, and to reforms to bring about equitable access to all South Africa's natural resources; and
(b) property is not limited to land.
(5) The state must take reasonable legislative and other measures, within its available resources, to foster conditions which enable citizens to gain access to land on an equitable basis.
(6) A person or community whose tenure of land is legally insecure as a result of past racially discriminatory laws or practices is entitled, to the extent provided by an Act of Parliament, either to tenure which is legally secure or to comparable redress.
(7) A person or community dispossessed of property after 19 June 1913 as a result of past racially discriminatory laws or practices is entitled, to the extent provided by an Act of Parliament, either to restitution of that property or to equitable redress.
(8) No provision of this section may impede the state from taking legislative and other measures to achieve land, water and related reform, in order to redress the results of past racial discrimination, provided that any departure from the provisions of this section is in accordance with the provisions of section 36 (1).
(9) Parliament must enact the legislation referred to in subsection (6).

## Housing

26. (1) Everyone has the right to have access to adequate housing.
(2) The state must take reasonable legislative and other measures, within its available resources, to achieve the progressive realisation of this right.
(3) No one may be evicted from their home, or have their home demolished, without an order of court made after considering all the relevant circumstances. No legislation may permit arbitrary evictions.

## Health care, food, water and social security

27. (1) Everyone has the right to have access to –
(a) health care services, including reproductive health care;
(b) sufficient food and water; and
(c) social security, including, if they are unable to support themselves and their dependants, appropriate social assistance.
(2) The state must take reasonable legislative and other measures, within its available resources, to achieve the progressive realisation of each of these rights.
(3) No one may be refused emergency medical treatment.

## Children

28. (1) Every child has the right –
(a) to a name and a nationality from birth;
(b) to family care or parental care, or to appropriate alternative care when removed from the family environment;
(c) to basic nutrition, shelter, basic health care services and social services;
(d) to be protected from maltreatment, neglect, abuse or degradation;
(e) to be protected from exploitative labour practices;
(f) not to be required or permitted to perform work or provide services that –
(i) are inappropriate for a person of that child's age; or
(ii) place at risk the child's well-being, education, physical or mental health or spiritual, moral or social development;
(g) not to be detained except as a measure of last resort, in which case, in addition to the rights a child enjoys under sections 12 and 35, the child may be detained only for the shortest appropriate period of time, and has the right to be –
(i) kept separately from detained persons over the age of 18 years; and
(ii) treated in a manner, and kept in conditions, that take account of the child's age;
(h) to have a legal practitioner assigned to the child by the state, and at state expense, in civil proceedings affecting the child, if substantial injustice would otherwise result; and
(i) not to be used directly in armed conflict, and to be protected in times of armed conflict.
(2) A child's best interests are of paramount importance in every matter concerning the child.
(3) In this section "child" means a person under the age of 18 years.

## Education

29. (1) Everyone has the right –
(a) to a basic education, including adult basic education; and
(b) to further education, which the state, through reasonable measures, must make progressively available and accessible.
(2) Everyone has the right to receive education in the official language or languages of their choice in public educational institutions where that education is reasonably practicable. In order to ensure the effective access to, and implementation of, this right, the state must consider all reasonable educational alternatives, including single medium institutions, taking into account –
(a) equity;
(b) practicability; and
(c) the need to redress the results of past racially discriminatory laws and practices.
(3) Everyone has the right to establish and maintain, at their own expense, independent educational institutions that –
(a) do not discriminate on the basis of race;
(b) are registered with the state; and
(c) maintain standards that are not inferior to standards at comparable public educational institutions.
(4) Subsection (3) does not preclude state subsidies for independent educational institutions.

## Language and culture

30. Everyone has the right to use the language and to participate in the cultural life of their choice, but no one exercising these rights may do so in a manner inconsistent with any provision of the Bill of Rights.

## Cultural, religious and linguistic communities

31. (1) Persons belonging to a cultural, religious or linguistic community may not be denied the right, with other members of that community –
(a) to enjoy their culture, practise their religion and use their language; and
(b) to form, join and maintain cultural, religious and linguistic associations and other organs of civil society.
(2) The rights in subsection (1) may not be exercised in a manner inconsistent with any provision of the Bill of Rights.

## Access to information

32. (1) Everyone has the right of access to –
(a) any information held by the state; and
(b) any information that is held by another person and that is required for the exercise or protection of any rights.
(2) National legislation must be enacted to give effect to this right, and may provide for reasonable measures to alleviate the administrative and financial burden on the state.

## Just administrative action

33. (1) Everyone has the right to administrative action that is lawful, reasonable and procedurally fair.
(2) Everyone whose rights have been adversely affected by administrative action has the right to be given written reasons.
(3) National legislation must be enacted to give effect to these rights, and must –
(a) provide for the review of administrative action by a court or, where appropriate, an independent and impartial tribunal;
(b) impose a duty on the state to give effect to the rights in subsections (1) and (2); and
(c) promote an efficient administration.

## Access to courts

34. Everyone has the right to have any dispute that can be resolved by the application of law decided in a fair public hearing before a court or, where appropriate, another independent and impartial tribunal or forum.

## Arrested, detained and accused persons

35. (1) Everyone who is arrested for allegedly committing an offence has the right –
(a) to remain silent;
(b) to be informed promptly –
(i) of the right to remain silent; and
(ii) of the consequences of not remaining silent;
(c) not to be compelled to make any confession or admission that could be used in evidence against that person;
(d) to be brought before a court as soon as reasonably possible, but not later than –
(i) 48 hours after the arrest; or
(ii) the end of the first court day after the expiry of the 48 hours, if the 48 hours expire outside ordinary court hours or on a day which is not an ordinary court day;
(e) at the first court appearance after being arrested, to be charged or to be informed of the reason for the detention to continue, or to be released; and
(f) to be released from detention if the interests of justice permit, subject to reasonable conditions.
(2) Everyone who is detained, including every sentenced prisoner, has the right –
(a) to be informed promptly of the reason for being detained;
(b) to choose, and to consult with, a legal practitioner, and to be informed of this right promptly;
(c) to have a legal practitioner assigned to the detained person by the state and at state expense, if substantial injustice would otherwise result, and to be informed of this right promptly;
(d) to challenge the lawfulness of the detention in person before a court and, if the detention is unlawful, to be released;
(e) to conditions of detention that are consistent with human dignity, including at least exercise and the provision, at state expense, of adequate accommodation, nutrition, reading material and medical treatment; and
(f) to communicate with, and be visited by, that person's –
(i) spouse or partner;
(ii) next of kin;
(iii) chosen religious counsellor; and
(iv) chosen medical practitioner.
(3) Every accused person has a right to a fair trial, which includes the right –
(a) to be informed of the charge with sufficient detail to answer it;
(b) to have adequate time and facilities to prepare a defence;
(c) to a public trial before an ordinary court;
(d) to have their trial begin and conclude without unreasonable delay;
(e) to be present when being tried;
(f) to choose, and be represented by, a legal practitioner, and to be informed of this right promptly;
(g) to have a legal practitioner assigned to the accused person by the state and at state expense, if substantial injustice would otherwise result, and to be informed of this right promptly;
(h) to be presumed innocent, to remain silent, and not to testify during the proceedings;
(i) to adduce and challenge evidence;
(j) not to be compelled to give self-incriminating evidence;
(k) to be tried in a language that the accused person understands or, if that is not practicable, to have the proceedings interpreted in that language;
(l) not to be convicted for an act or omission that was not an offence under either national or international law at the time it was committed or omitted;
(m) not to be tried for an offence in respect of an act or omission for which that person has previously been either acquitted or convicted;
(n) to the benefit of the least severe of the prescribed punishments if the prescribed punishment for the offence has been changed between the time that the offence was committed and the time of sentencing; and
(o) of appeal to, or review by, a higher court.
(4) Whenever this section requires information to be given to a person, that information must be given in a language that the person understands.
(5) Evidence obtained in a manner that violates any right in the Bill of Rights must be excluded if the admission of that evidence would render the trial unfair or otherwise be detrimental to the administration of justice.

## Limitation of rights

36. (1) The rights in the Bill of Rights may be limited only in terms of law of general application to the extent that the limitation is reasonable and justifiable in an open and democratic society based on human dignity, equality and freedom, taking into account all relevant factors, including –
(a) the nature of the right;
(b) the importance of the purpose of the limitation;
(c) the nature and extent of the limitation;
(d) the relation between the limitation and its purpose; and
(e) less restrictive means to achieve the purpose.
(2) Except as provided in subsection (1) or in any other provision of the Constitution, no law may limit any right entrenched in the Bill of Rights.

## States of emergency

37. (1) A state of emergency may be declared only in terms of an Act of Parliament, and only when –
(a) the life of the nation is threatened by war, invasion, general insurrection, disorder, natural disaster or other public emergency; and
(b) the declaration is necessary to restore peace and order.
(2) A declaration of a state of emergency, and any legislation enacted or other action taken in consequence of that declaration, may be effective only –
(a) prospectively; and
(b) for no more than 21 days from the date of the declaration, unless the National Assembly resolves to extend the declaration. The Assembly may extend a declaration of a state of emergency for no more than three months at a time. The first extension of the state of emergency must be by a resolution adopted with a supporting vote of a majority of the members of the Assembly. Any subsequent extension must be by a resolution adopted with a supporting vote of at least 60 per cent of the members of the Assembly. A resolution in terms of this paragraph may be adopted only following a public debate in the Assembly.
(3) Any competent court may decide on the validity of –
(a) a declaration of a state of emergency;
(b) any extension of a declaration of a state of emergency; or
(c) any legislation enacted, or other action taken, in consequence of a declaration of a state of emergency.
(4) Any legislation enacted in consequence of a declaration of a state of emergency may derogate from the Bill of Rights only to the extent that –
(a) the derogation is strictly required by the emergency; and
(b) the legislation –
(i) is consistent with the Republic's obligations under international law applicable to states of emergency;
(ii) conforms to subsection (5); and
(iii) is published in the national Government Gazette as soon as reasonably possible after being enacted.
(5) No Act of Parliament that authorises a declaration of a state of emergency, and no legislation enacted or other action taken in consequence of a declaration, may permit or authorise –
(a) indemnifying the state, or any person, in respect of any unlawful act;
(b) any derogation from this section; or
(c) any derogation from a section mentioned in column 1 of the Table of Non-Derogable Rights, to the extent indicated opposite that section in column 3 of the Table.

### Table of Non-Derogable Rights

| 1<br>SECTION NUMBER | 2<br>SECTION TITLE | 3<br>EXTENT TO WHICH THE RIGHT IS PROTECTED |
|---|---|---|
| 9 | Equality | With respect to unfair discrimination solely on the grounds of race, colour, ethnic or social origin, sex, religion or language |
| 10 | Human dignity | Entirely |
| 11 | Life | Entirely |
| 12 | Freedom and security of the person | With respect to subsections (1) (d) and (e) and 2 (c) |
| 13 | Slavery, servitude and forced labour | With respect to slavery and servitude |
| 28 | Children | With respect to:<br>– subsection (1) (d) and (e);<br>– the rights in subparagraphs (i) and (ii) of subsection (1) (g); and<br>– subsection (1) (i) in respect of children of 15 years and younger. |
| 35 | Arrested, detained and accused persons | With respect to:<br>– subsections (1) (a), (b) and (c) and (2) (d);<br>– the rights in paragraphs (a) to (o) of subsection (3), excluding paragraph (d);<br>– subsection (4); and<br>– subsection (5) with respect to the exclusion of evidence if the admission of that evidence would render the trial unfair. |

(6) Whenever anyone is detained without trial in consequence of a derogation of rights resulting from a declaration of a state of emergency, the following conditions must be observed:
(a) An adult family member or friend of the detainee must be contacted as soon as reasonably possible, and informed that the person has been detained.
(b) A notice must be published in the national Government Gazette within five days of the person being detained, stating the detainee's name and place of detention and referring to the emergency measure in terms of which that person has been detained.
(c) The detainee must be allowed to choose, and be visited at any reasonable time by, a medical practitioner.
(d) The detainee must be allowed to choose, and be visited at any reasonable time by, a legal representative.
(e) A court must review the detention as soon as reasonably possible, but no later than 10 days after the date the person was detained, and the court must release the detainee unless it is necessary to continue the detention to restore peace and order.
(f) A detainee who is not released in terms of a review under paragraph (e), or who is not released in terms of a review under this paragraph, may apply to a court for a further review of the detention at any time after 10 days have passed since the previous review, and the court must release the detainee unless it is still necessary to continue the detention to restore peace and order.
(g) The detainee must be allowed to appear in person before any court considering the detention, to be represented by a legal practitioner at those hearings, and to make representations against continued detention.
(h) The state must present written reasons to the court to justify the continued detention of the detainee, and must give a copy of those reasons to the detainee at least two days before the court reviews the detention.
(7) If a court releases a detainee, that person may not be detained again on the same grounds unless the state first shows a court good cause for re-detaining that person.
(8) Subsections (6) and (7) do not apply to persons who are not South African citizens and who are detained in consequence of an international armed conflict. Instead, the state must comply with the standards binding on the Republic under international humanitarian law in respect of the detention of such persons.

## Enforcement of rights

38. Anyone listed in this section has the right to approach a competent court, alleging that a right in the Bill of Rights has been infringed or threatened, and the court may grant appropriate relief, including a declaration of rights. The persons who may approach a court are –
(a) anyone acting in their own interest;
(b) anyone acting on behalf of another person who cannot act in their own name;
(c) anyone acting as a member of, or in the interest of, a group or class of persons;
(d) anyone acting in the public interest; and
(h) an association acting in the interest of its members.

## Interpretation of Bill of Rights

39. (1) When interpreting the Bill of Rights, a court, tribunal or forum –
(a) must promote the values that underlie an open and democratic society based on human dignity, equality and freedom;
(b) must consider international law; and
(c) may consider foreign law.
(2) When interpreting any legislation, and when developing the common law or customary law, every court, tribunal or forum must promote the spirit, purport and objects of the Bill of Rights.
(3) The Bill of Rights does not deny the existence of any other rights or freedoms that are recognised or conferred by common law, customary law or legislation, to the extent that they are consistent with the Bill.

Cyril Ramaphosa

Arthur Chaskalson

Presented by The Constitutional Court of South Africa

Roelf Meyer

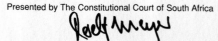

# Bibliography

Andrews, P and Ellmann, S (eds) (2001) *The Post-Apartheid Constitutions: Perspectives on South Africa's Basic Law,* Witwatersrand University Press, Johannesburg

Bernstein, R (1999) *Memory Against Forgetting: Memoirs from a Life in South African Politics, 1938–1964,* Viking Press, New York

Bizos, G (2009) *Odyssey to Freedom,* Struik Publishers, Johannesburg

Bunting, B (1975) *Moses Kotane: South African Revolutionary, A Political Biography,* Inkululeko Publications, London, www.marxists.org

Butler, A (2008) *Cyril Ramaphosa,* Jacana Media, Johannesburg

Crafford, FS (2005) *Jan Smuts: A Biography,* Kessinger Publishing Co., USA

Cock, J (1997) 'Women in SA's transition to Democracy', in J Scott, C Kaplan and D Keats (eds) *Transitions, Environments, Translations: Feminism in International Politics,* Routledge, New York

Coleman, M (ed.) (1998) *A Crime Against Humanity: Analysing the Repression of the Apartheid State,* Human Rights Committee, Johannesburg

Constitutional Court Publication (2005) *The Constitutional Court: The First Ten Years,* Johannesburg

Cornell, D and Muvangua, N (eds) (2010) *Law in the uBuntu of South Africa,* isthisseattaken.co.za

Davenport, T (1991) *South Africa: A Modern History,* 4th ed., Macmillan, London

De Klerk, FW (2000) *The Last Trek – A New Beginning: The Autobiography,* Pan Macmillan, London

Doxtader, E (2009) *With Faith in the Works of Words: The beginnings of reconciliation in South Africa, 1985–1995,* David Philip Publishers, Cape Town

Ebrahim, H (1998) *Soul of the Nation: Constitution-making in South Africa,* Oxford University Press, Cape Town

Frederikse, J (1990) *The Unbreakable Thread: Non-racialism in South Africa,* Ravan Press, Johannesburg

Friedman, S (ed.) (1993) *The Long Journey: South Africa's quest for a negotiated settlement,* Ravan Press, Johannesburg

Gevisser, M (2009) *Thabo Mbeki: The Dream Deferred,* Jonathan Ball Publishers, Johannesburg

Giliomee, H and Mbenga, B (2007) *New History of South Africa,* Tafelberg Publishers, Cape Town

Gloppen, S (1997) *South Africa: The Battle over the Constitution,* Dartmouth Publishing Company, Aldershot, UK

Hancock, W and Van der Poel, J (2007) *Selections from the Smuts Papers: Volume 1, June 1886–May 1902,* Cambridge University Press, London

Karis, T and Carter, G (eds) (1972) *From Protest to Challenge: A Documentary History of African Politics in South Africa, 1882–1964, Volume 2, Hope and Challenge,* Hoover Institution Press, Stanford University, California (published online by SAHO)

Leon, T (2008) *On the Contrary: Leading the opposition in the new South Africa,* Jonathan Ball Publishers, Cape Town

Lodge, T (1983) *Black Politics in South Africa Since 1945,* Longman, London

Marks, S and Trapido, S (1987) *The Politics of Race, Class and Nationalism in Twentieth-century South Africa,* Longman, London

Mandela, N (1995) *Long Walk to Freedom; The Autobiography of Nelson Mandela,* Little Brown & Co., London

Mbeki, G (1964) *South Africa: The Peasants' Revolt,* www.anc.org.za

McKendrick, B and Hoffmann, W (1990) *People and Violence in South Africa,* Oxford University Press, Cape Town

Nicol, M (1997) *The Making of the Constitution,* Churchill Murray Publications, Cape Town

Odendaal, A (1984) *Vukani Bantu! The Beginnings of Black Protest Politics in South Africa to 1912,* David Philip Publishers, Cape Town

Reader's Digest (1995) *Illustrated History of South Africa: The Real Story,* The Reader's Digest Association Limited, Cape Town

Saunders, J (2006) *Apartheid's Friends: The Rise and Fall of South Africa's Secret Service,* Jonathan Ball Publishers, Johannesburg

Sisk, T (1995) *Democratisation in South Africa: The Elusive Social Contract,* Princeton University Press, USA

South African Democracy Education Trust (2004) *The Road to Democracy in South Africa, Volume 1, 1970–1980,* Mutloatse Arts Heritage Trust/Zebra Press, Cape Town

Slovo, J (1995) *Slovo: The Unfinished Autobiography,* Ravan Press, Johannesburg

Sparks, A (1994) *Tomorrow is Another Country: The inside story of South Africa's negotiated revolution,* Struik Publishers, Johannesburg

Sparks, A (2003) *Beyond the Miracle: Inside the new South Africa,* University of Chicago Press, Chicago

Spitz, R and Chaskalson, M (2000) *The Politics of Transition: A hidden history of South Africa's negotiated settlement,* Witwatersrand University Press, Johannesburg

Thompson, L (1985) *The Political Mythology of Apartheid,* Yale University Press, New Haven

Waldheimer, P (1998) *Anatomy of a Miracle: The End of Apartheid and the Birth of a New South Africa,* Rutgers University Press, New Brunswick

Zapiro (2009) *The Mandela Files,* Double Storey, Cape Town

## Journal and Newspaper Articles

Anderson, A (2003) 'Restorative Justice: The African philosophy of Ubuntu and the diversion of criminal prosecution', www.isrcl.org

Barnes, C and De Klerk, E (2002) 'South Africa's multi-party constitutional negotiation process', Conciliation Resources, London, www.c-r.org

Belani, A (2004) 'The South African Constitutional Court's decision in TAC: A "reasonable choice"', www.thegovernancecommons.org

Budlender, G (2002) 'Lessons from Grootboom', unpublished paper, www.escrnet.org/caselaw

Carpenter, G (1994) 'The Republic of South Africa Constitution Act 200 of 1993: An overview', SAPL 9, p. 222 at 227

Edgar, R (1995) 'Muziwakhe Lembede and African Nationalism', Seminar Paper, Institute for Advanced Social Research, University of the Witwatersrand, Johannesburg

Feinberg, H (2006) 'Protest in South Africa: Prominent Black Leaders' Commentary on the Natives Land Act, 1913-1936', Historia, 52, 2

Forbath, WE (2008) 'Realising a Constitutional Social Right: Cultural Transformation, Deep Institutional Reform, and the Roles of Advocacy and Adjudication', Public Law Research Paper No. 149, University of Texas Law, ssrn.com/abstract

Giliomee, H (2008) 'Great Expectations: President PW Botha's Rubicon speech of 1985', www.newhistory.co.za

Idowu, W and Oke, M (2008) 'Theories of Law and Morality: Perspectives from Contemporary African Jurisprudence', In-Spire Journal of Law, Politics and Societies, Vol. 3 No. 2, www.in-spire.org

Kahanowitz, S (2009) 'Economic and Social Rights: Reflection to Celebrate the 60th Anniversary of the Declaration of Human Rights', Maryland Journal of International Law, Vol. 24: 244

Kallaway, P (1974) 'FS Malan, the Cape Liberal Tradition, and South African Politics, 1908-1924', The Journal of African History, Vol. 15, No. 1, South African Historical Society/Unisa Press, Pretoria

Liebenberg, S (2005) 'The value of human dignity in interpreting socio-economic rights', SAJHR 1 173, www.isrcl.org/papers/anderson

Maharaj, M (2008) 'The ANC and South Africa's Negotiated Transition to Democracy and Peace', Berghof Series Resistance/Liberation Movements and Transition to Politics, www.berghofconflictresearch.org

McCrudden, C (2008) 'Human Dignity and Judicial Interpretation of Human Rights', European Journal of International Law, Oxford Legal Studies Research Paper No. 24/2008, www.oxfordjournals.org

Mokgoro, JY (2009) 'Ubuntu and The Law in South Africa', www.ajol.info

Mokgoro, JY (2010) 'Judicial Appointments', Paper at the Middle Temple and South Africa Conference: Judicial Independence, www.sabar.co.za

Monroe, R (1984) 'Lessons of the 1950s', Inqaba Ya Basebenzi, 13, March-May, www.marxist.com

Moseneke, D (2011) 'Striking a Balance', Sunday Times, 2 October 2011

Msimang, S (1936) 'The Crisis', sahistory.org.za

Ndebele, N (2011) 'Our Dream is Turning Sour', Sunday Times, 25 September 2011

Phala, KAR (2009) 'Celebrating and commemorating twenty years of the Harare Declaration', www.sahistory.org.za

Pillay, GJ (1993) 'Albert Luthuli, Voices of Liberation', HSRC Printers, Pretoria

Quint, P (2009) 'The Universal Declaration and South African constitutional law: A response to Justice Arthur Chaskalson', www.digitalcommons.law.umaryland.ed

Sachs, A (undated) 'Notes towards Memoirs', Mayibuye Archives, Cape Town

Seehaam, S (2008) 'Evictions: Towards a transformative interpretation of the constitutional requirement of considering "all relevant circumstances"', www.ru.ac.za

Seme, P (1911) 'Native Union', Imvo Zabantsundu, 24 October 1911, King William's Town

Stuart, W (2009) 'Breaking the Tie: Evictions from private land, homelessness and new normality', SALJ, 9, www.abahlali.org

'The Constitutional Mandate: Dynamic and pro-Active Legislatures', www.publiclaw.uct.ac.za

The National Party Government (1992) 'Proposals on Fundamental Rights', Modern Law Review, 57

Van der Vyver, JD (1989) 'The Democratic Draft Bill of Rights: "Freedom under the Rule of Law" - Advancing Liberty in the New South Africa', South African Journal for Human Rights, SAJHR, 133, May 1993

Venter, F (1995) 'Requirements for a New Constitutional Text: The Imperatives of the Constitutional Principles', SALJ, 32

## Websites

www.anc.org.za
www.constitutionalcourt.org.za
www.constitutionallyspeaking.co.za
www.georgetown.edu/guides/southafricanlegalresearch.cfm
www.joburg.org.za
www.mg.co.za
www.nelsonmandela.org/omalley
www.news.findlaw.com/
www.olivescreinerletters.ed.ac.uk
www.politicsweb.co.za/politicsweb/
www.saflii.org/za
www.sahistory.org.za/
www.sacp.org.za/index.php
www.tac.org.za
www.wiredspace.wits.ac.za

## Position Papers/Speeches

'Accord on Afrikaner self-determination', 23 April 1994, www.nelsonmandela.org/omalley

ANC (1943) 'Africans' Claims in South Africa' including 'The Atlantic Charter from the Standpoint of Africans within the Union of South Africa' and 'Bill of Rights' adopted by the ANC Annual Conference, ANC Historical Documents Archive and Historical Papers, ANC, Box 1

ANC (1955) 'The Freedom Charter', ANC Historical Documents Archive, www.anc.org.za

ANC (1961) 'Resolution of the All-In African Conference held in Pietermaritzburg', 25-26 March 1961, ANC Historical Documents Archive, www.anc.org.za

ANC (1961) MK Manifesto, ANC Historical Documents Archive, www.anc. org.za

ANC (1969) 'Forward to Freedom: Strategy, tactics and programme of the African National Congress, South Africa', adopted at the Morogoro Conference, Tanzania, ANC Historical Documents Archive, www.anc. org.za

ANC (1989) 'Declaration of the OAU Ad-Hoc Committee on Southern Africa on the Question of South Africa' known as the 'Harare Declaration', 21 August 1989, ANC Historical Documents Archive, www.anc.org.za

ANC (1990) 'National Consultative Conference: Resolutions for the coming year', December 1990, Historical Papers, AG 2510, Box 1, A.2.2.2.1

ANC (1991) 'Advance to National Democracy: Strategy and Tactics of the ANC', February 1991, Historical Papers, AG 2510, Box 1, A.2.2.3.5

ANC (1992) 'Negotiations: A Strategic Perspective', 25 November 1992, ANC Historical Documents Archive, www.anc.org.za

Codesa 1 (1991) 'Declaration of Intent', 21 December 1991, National Archives, Pretoria

De Klerk, FW (1990) 'Opening Address to Parliament', 2 February 1990, De Klerk Foundation

De Klerk, FW (1992) 'Reply to Nelson's Mandela Memorandum', 2 July 1992

De Klerk, FW (2011) 'The Constitution Requirements for Sustainable Development', Sun City, 2 July 1992

IFP (1992) 'Position Paper of the Inkatha Freedom Party', February 1992

Interim Constitution (1993) 'Constitutional Principles, Schedule 4, Act 200 of 1993'

IFP, ANC, NP (1994) 'Memorandum of the Agreement for Reconciliation and Peace Between the IFP, the ANC and the South African Government', www.nelsonmandela.org/omalley

Jabavu, D et al (1935) Native Views on the Native Bills, Lovedale Press

Luthuli, A (1957) 'Letter from Chief Albert J Luthuli to Prime Minister JG Strijdom suggesting a multi-racial convention', 28 May 1957, Historical Papers, University of the Witwatersrand, Johannesburg

Mandela, N (1961) 'First Letter From Nelson Mandela to Hendrik Verwoed', 20 April 1961, www.nelsonmandela.org/omalley

Mandela, N (1961) 'Second Letter From Nelson Mandela to Hendrik Verwoerd', 26 June 1961, www.nelsonmandela.org/omalley

Mandela, N (1961) 'Letters from Nelson Mandela to Sir De Villiers Graaff, leader of the United Party', 23 May 1961, www.anc.org.za

Mandela, N (1989) 'Notes prepared by Nelson Mandela for his meeting with PW Botha', 5 July 1989, Nelson Mandela Foundation

Mandela, N (1990) 'Speech at the Grand Parade after his release', Grand Parade, Cape Town, 11 February 1990, www.anc.org.za

Mandela, N (1994) 'Speech announcing the ANC Election Victory', Johannesburg, 2 May 1994, www.anc.org.za

Mandela, N (1994) 'Speech at Presidential Inauguration', Union Buildings, Pretoria, 10 May 1994, www.anc.org.za

Mandela, N (1989) 'A Document to Create A Climate of Understanding: Nelson Mandela to FW de Klerk', 12 December 1989, www.e-tools.co.za/ anc/mandela/nm891212.html

Mandela, N (1992) 'Memorandum from Nelson Mandela for FW de Klerk', 26 June 1992, National Archives, Pretoria

Mbeki, T (2004) 'Speech at the Opening of the Constitutional Court building', 21 March 2004, Braamfontein

Msimang, RW (1913) 'Natives Land Act 1913: Specific Cases of Evictions and Hardships, etc.', Friends of South Africa Library, Cape Town

Parliamentary Debates (1910-1994), Parliament Library, Cape Town

Resolution by the Conference for a Democratic Future on Negotiations and the Constitutional Assembly, 8 December 1989

'Record of Understanding', 26 September 1992, www.nelsonmandela. org/omalley

'Resolution on the need for the resumption of multi-party negotiations', 5 March 1993, www.nelsonmandela.org/omalley

SACP (1929) 'Programme of the SACP as adopted at the Seventh Congress, 1929', www.sacp.org.za

'The DF Malan Accord', 12 February 1991, www.nelsonmandela.org/ omalley

'The Groote Schuur Minute', 4 May 1990, www.nelsonmandela.org/ omalley

The Negotiation Forum (1993) 'Resolution on Violence', 1 April 1993, South African History Archive

'The Pretoria Minute', 6 August 1990, www.nelsonmandela.org/omalley

## Filmography

Jammy, D and Gavshon, H (1996) The Deadline, Curious Pictures for the Mail & Guardian

Jammy, D and Gavshon, H (2006) After The Deadline, Curious Pictures

## Archival Collections

Albie Sachs Collection, Mayibuye Archive, University of the Western Cape

ANC Early Archives, Historical Papers, University of the Witwatersrand

ANC Constitutional Assembly Archives, University of Fort Hare

Codesa Collection, National Archives, Pretoria

Constitutional Assembly Collection, National Archives, Pretoria

Cyril Ramaphosa Collection, University of Fort Hare

Francois Venter Collection, Constitutional Court Library, Johannesburg

Hassen Ebrahim, Private Collection, Pretoria

Joe Slovo Collection, South African History Archives, University of the Witwatersrand, Johannesburg

Nelson Mandela Collection, Nelson Mandela Centre of Memory, Johannesburg

Office of the ANC President, Nelson Mandela Papers, 1983-1994, University of Fort Hare

UDF and ANC Poster Collection, South African History Archives, University of the Witwatersrand

## Interviews

Dorsey, E (1992) Interview with Professor Albie Sachs, Georgia State University Newspapers, USA

Interview transcripts with Colin Eglin, Valli Moosa, Baleka Kgositsile, Piet Marais, Roelf Meyer, Blade Nzimande, Dene Smuts, Constand Viljoen, Leon Wessels, from the documentaries *The Deadline* and *After The Deadline*, Curious Pictures for the *Mail & Guardian*

Interview transcripts with Sheila Camerer, Cheryl Carolus, Kobie Coetzee, Tertius Delport, FW de Klerk, Dawie de Villiers, Mac Maharaj, Valli Moosa, Corne Mulder, Cyril Ramaphosa, Leon Wessels from O'Malley, P (1990-7) The *Heart of Hope: South Africa's Transition from Apartheid to Democracy*, University of the Western Cape and University of Massachusetts, Boston, www.nelsonmandela.org/omalley

Cort, S and Segal, L (2011) Interview with former Chief Justice, Arthur Chaskalson, Johannesburg

Cort, S and Segal, L (2011) Interview with Justice Kriegler, Johannesburg

Cort, S and Segal, L (2011) Interview with Wim Trengove, Johannesburg

Segal, L (2011) Interview with Claire Avidon and Lwanda Xaso, Johannesburg

Segal, L (2011) Interview with Kate O'Regan, Cape Town

Segal, L (2011) Interview with Cyril Ramaphosa, Johannesburg

## Court Cases

In the Constitutional Court of South Africa, Certification of the Constitution of the Republic of South Africa, 1996, case no. CCT 23/96, judgement delivered on 6 September 1996

In the Constitutional Court of South Africa, in the matter between The Premier of KwaZulu-Natal and others, and The President of the Republic of South Africa and others, case no. CCT 36/95, judgement delivered on 29 November 1995

In the Constitutional Court of South Africa, in the matter of *August and Another v The Independent Electoral Commission (IEC) and Others,* case no. CCT8/99, judgement delivered on 1 April 1999

In the Constitutional Court of South Africa, in the matter of *Alexkor Limited v The Richtersveld Community and Others,* case no. CCT 19/03, judgement delivered on 14 October 2003

In the Constitutional Court of South Africa, in the matter of *Carmichele v The Minister of Safety and Security and the Minister of Justice and Constitutional Development,* case no. CCT 48/00, judgement delivered on 16 August 2001

In the Constitutional Court of South Africa, in the matter of *Grootboom and Others v Government of the Republic of South Africa,* case no. CCT 11/00, judgement delivered on 26 September 2000

In the Constitutional Court of South Africa, in the matter of *Hoffmann v South African Airways,* case no. CCT 17/00, judgement delivered on 28 September 2000

In the Constitutional Court, in the matter of *The Minister of Home Affairs and Another v Fourie and Others,* case no. CCT60/04 and *Lesbian and Gay Equality Project v Minister of Home Affairs and Others,* case no. CCT10/05, judgement delivered on 1 December 2005

In the Constitutional Court of South Africa, in the matter of *The State v Makwanyane and Another,* case no. CCT3/94, judgement delivered on 6 June 1995

In the Constitutional Court of South Africa, in the matter of *Minister of Health and Others v Treatment Action Campaign and Others (1),* case no. CCT 9/02, judgement delivered on 5 July 2002

## Photographic Archives

Africa Media Online
Avusa Library
Bailey's African History Archives
Corbis online gallery
Gallo Images
Magnum Photos
Oryx Multimedia
Reuters
UN Photograph Library
UWC / Robben Island / Mayibuye Archives

# List of Abbreviations

| | |
|---|---|
| ANC | African National Congress |
| ANCYL | ANC Youth League |
| AWB | Afrikaner Weerstandsbeweging (Afrikaner Resistance Movement) |
| AZAPO | Azanian People's Organisation |
| BCM | Black Consciousness Movement |
| CA | Constitutional Assembly |
| CODESA | Convention for a Democratic South Africa |
| CONTRALESA | Congress of Traditional Leaders of South Africa |
| COSAG | Concerned South Africans Group |
| COSAS | Congress of South African Students |
| COSATU | Congress of South African Trade Unions |
| CP | Conservative Party |
| CP | Constitutional Principles |
| CPRC | Coloured Persons' Representative Council |
| CPSA | Communist Party of South Africa |
| DP | Democratic Party |
| FC | Freedom Charter |
| FF | Freedom Front |
| GNU | Government of National Unity |
| IC | Interim Constitution |
| ICU | Industrial and Commercial Workers' Union of South Africa |
| IEC | Independent Electoral Commission |
| IFP | Inkatha Freedom Party |
| JSC | Judicial Service Commission |
| MDM | Mass Democratic Movement |
| MPNP | Multi-Party Negotiation Process |
| MK | Umkhonto we Sizwe (the military wing of the African National Congress) |
| MP | Member of Parliament |
| MPNP | Multi Party Negotiating Forum |
| NEC | National Executive Committee (of the ANC) |
| NIS | National Intelligence Service |
| NGO | Non-Government Organisation |
| NP | National Party |
| PAC | Pan Africanist Congress |
| RMC | Release Mandela Campaign |
| RSA | Republic of South Africa |
| SACP | South African Communist Party |
| SADF | South African Defence Force |
| SANNC | South African Native National Congress |
| TBVC | Transkei, Bophuthatswana, Venda and Ciskei (the independent Bantustans) |
| TEC | Transitional Executive Council |
| TRC | Truth and Reconciliation Commission |
| UDF | United Democratic Front |
| UDM | United Democratic Movement |

CALIFORNIA
ANGELS

AL WEST

RICHARD RAMBECK

Published by Creative Education, Inc.

123 S. Broad Street, Mankato, Minnesota 56001

Art Director, Rita Marshall
Cover and title page design by Virginia Evans
Cover and title page illustration by Rob Day
Type set by FinalCopy Electronic Publishing
Book design by Rita Marshall

Photos by Tom Dipace, Duomo, Focus on Sports,
FPG, Michael Ponzini, Bruce Schwartzman,
UPI/Bettmann, Ron Vesley and Wide World Photos

**Library of Congress Cataloging-in-Publication Data**

Rambeck, Richard.

California Angels / by Richard Rambeck.

p.   cm.

Summary: A team history of one of the Los Angeles
area's two baseball teams, the Angels, born in 1961,
and owned by former movie cowboy Gene Autry.

ISBN 0-88682-449-4

1. California Angels (Baseball team)—History—
Juvenile literature.   [1. California Angels (Baseball
team)—History.   2. Baseball—History.]   I. Title.
GV875.C34R36   1991                        91-2478
796.357'64'0979494—dc20                    CIP

## THE EARLY YEARS

**W**ith approximately thirty million residents, California is, by far, the most populous state in the nation. The place known as the Golden State has ten million more people than any other state. About three-fourths of the residents of California live within 150 miles of the city of Los Angeles, the nation's second largest city. Los Angeles, which has more than three million residents now, had only one hundred thousand in 1900.

Given this population explosion, it's not surprising that the Los Angeles area is home to not one, but two major-league baseball teams. L.A.'s first major-league club was the Los Angeles Dodgers, who moved west from

*An original member of the Angels, Ken McBride.*

**1 9 6 0**

*Gene Autry, ("The Singing Cowboy"), purchased interest in the new expansion team the Los Angeles Angels.*

Brooklyn in 1957. The second team was the Los Angeles Angels, founded in 1961 as an expansion team in the American League. The Angels, however, didn't stay long in Los Angeles. Before the start of the 1966 season, the newly named California Angels moved south from Los Angeles to a new stadium in Anaheim, California, a growing city about thirty miles from L.A. Anaheim is best known as the home of Disneyland, which is about two miles from where the California Angels play in beautiful Anaheim Stadium.

The Angels have had many successful years in Anaheim. The franchise also posted solid records while based in Los Angeles. In the club's first year, 1961, it set a record for victories by a first-year expansion team. The following season the upstart Angels roared to the top of the American League early in the year. Amazingly, the second-year club was in first place on July 4. Historically, the team in first place on Independence Day has often gone on to win the pennant; the Angels, however, faded to third by the end of the season, still a remarkable performance for a new team.

The Angels slumped to a ninth-place finish in 1963, but the team had started to lay the groundwork for future success. The club paid $200,000 to sign Rick Reichart, a young outfielder. It was the largest bonus in the history of baseball up to that time. Such expensive signings were typical of the Angels and their flamboyant owner, Gene Autry, a former movie cowboy. Autry spared no expense in trying to build a championship team, and the Reichart signing was the first of several costly deals the Angels would make over the next three decades.

*Another Autry signing, outfielder Dante Bichette.*

## ANGELS GET A NEW CHANCE

*On May 5, big lefthander Bo Belinsky threw the Angels' first no-hit game.*

**L**ed by Reichart and a young pitcher named Wilmer Dean Chance, the Angels improved dramatically in 1964, finishing fifth in the league. Chance, a lanky lad from the horse country of Wayne County, Ohio, uncorked a pitching streak that tore apart the American League, winning twenty games and posting eleven shutouts. For his efforts Chance was presented the American League's Cy Young Award.

Unfortunately for the Angels, Chance was destined to leave the team. The cocky Chance demanded a big raise from the Angels, but even a spendthrift like Autry wasn't about to pay Chance what he was asking. Chance then complained about the team's "penny-pinching" ways to the newspapers, the fans, and anyone else who would listen. Finally, his bragging and complaining made everyone, including the other players on the team, unhappy. In December 1966 Chance was traded to the Minnesota Twins for outfielder Jimmie Hall, first baseman Don Mincher, and pitcher Pat Cimino.

Even without Chance the Angels remained a fairly decent team. The main reasons for this were Reichart, shortstop Jim Fregosi, and second baseman Bobby Knoop. However, the Angels needed more quality pitching. So they traded for a young, fire-balling pitcher who was known to have occasional problems with control. The pitcher was Nolan Ryan.

## THE RYAN EXPRESS STOPS IN CALIFORNIA

**R**yan began his major-league career with the New York Mets in 1969, the year the amazing Mets won the World Series. But unlike other promising young pitchers on the Mets staff, such as Tom Seaver, Jerry Koosman, and Gary Gentry, the often wild Ryan never found a home in New York. Ryan struggled as a part-time starter until being traded to the Angels in 1972. When the hard-throwing right-hander landed in the American League, he began to flourish, winning nineteen games for the Angels in his first year. He also had a sparkling ERA of 2.29, and his 329 strikeouts easily topped the league. But Ryan also walked 157 batters, threw eighteen wild pitches, and hit ten batters.

1 9 7 3

*In the final appearance of his record-setting season Nolan Ryan struck out 16 Minnesota batters.*

Ryan's wildness actually became one of his best weapons. "Nolan Ryan is the only man in baseball I'm afraid of," said slugger Reggie Jackson. "If he ever hits me," said Minnesota power hitter Harmon Killebrew, "I'll have him arrested for manslaughter."

In 1973 Ryan set a major-league record with 383 strikeouts. He also won twenty games and threw two no-hitters that season. "He's spectacular," said Herb Score, a pitcher for the Cleveland Indians in the 1950s. "With someone like Ryan, there is always the possibility of a no-hitter or a strikeout record. He is the kind of pitcher who draws fans. It's exciting to watch him."

It wasn't very exciting, however, for batters facing Ryan. Angels pitching coach Larry Sherry claimed that Ryan embarrassed hitters, "and they hate that. If you let him get a head of steam by the seventh inning, you can't hit him. You can't even *see* him."

Ryan had another great year in 1974, winning twenty-two games and throwing another no-hitter. During the 1975 season, however, he developed a sore arm which would bother him for several years. Despite the pain

*Current California ace Chuck Finley.*

*The legendary Reggie Jackson.*

*Although the Angels said hello to Carew, they said goodbye to Nolan Ryan (right), as he completed his last season in California.*

Ryan threw another no-hitter in 1975, the fourth in his career, which tied a major-league record.

Unfortunately for the Angels, their level of success didn't match Ryan's. Despite a solid pitching staff, the Angels weren't able to dislodge the powerful Oakland A's and Kansas City Royals from the top of the American League West Division. What the Angels needed to put them over the top was a great hitter, and during the 1979 season, they made a key trade that landed them one of the finest in baseball—Rod Carew.

### CAREW CRUISES AT THE PLATE

Carew, a first baseman, came to the Angels in a trade from the Minnesota Twins, and there was no doubt that he could hit. In fact, he had won the America League batting title in 1969, 1972, 1973, 1974, 1975, 1977, and 1978. He was known for his ability to adjust to all pitchers and all situations. Carew actually had several batting stances, and used them depending on how and where he wanted to hit the ball. "The man never wastes a time at bat," said Angel second baseman Bobby Grich. "I don't care if the score is 16–1 or 2–1. And he makes hitting look so effortless. You watch him, and you say to yourself, 'Boy, that looks easy.' Then you get up there and pop one up."

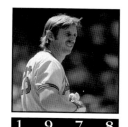

*California outfielder Joe Rudi launched an unbelievable three grand slams during the season.*

Carew believed the key to his success was his ability to remain loose at the plate. "I relax the upper part of my body," Carew said. "I don't squeeze the bat. If you do you lose flexibility. When the pitch comes, I can direct my bat in many ways."

Carew had an immediate impact on the Angels, but outfielder Don Baylor had an even bigger impact. Led by Baylor, who won the American League Most Valuable Player award, the Angels won the AL West Division title in 1979, their first-ever division championship. Baylor, who had a league-leading 139 runs batted in, was one of several ex-Baltimore Orioles who keyed California's offense. Grich and third baseman Doug DeCinces were other ex-Orioles who had excellent years in 1979. After winning the AL West, the Angels and their ex-Orioles faced the current Orioles in the American League Championship Series. Baltimore prevailed in the five-game playoff and advanced to the World Series.

Despite their success, the Angels and owner Gene Autry decided to make changes before the 1980 season. The biggest change was the trade of Nolan Ryan to the Houston Astros. Autry felt that Ryan, who was 16–14 in

*On September 25, Frank Tanana pitched a five-hit victory to clinch the Angels' first division title.*

1979, wasn't worth the price of a superstar. "Why, I can get two 8–7 pitchers for a fraction of what I'd have to pay him," Autry groused. The Angels owner wasn't afraid to spend money, however, to bring in players who could make the team a success. By the middle of the 1982 season, Autry had assembled a stable of former American League Most Valuable Players: Fred Lynn (Boston, 1975), Carew (Minnesota, 1977), Baylor (California, 1979), and Reggie Jackson (Oakland, 1973).

Led by these stars, the Angels stayed in contention for the AL West title all season. The home run was California's major weapon: Jackson hit thirty-six, DeCinces clubbed thirty, outfielder Brian Downing had twenty-eight, and Lynn hit twenty-one. In addition, those four players accounted for 368 RBI. The Angels also got great pitching from Geoff Zahn, who registered a career-high eighteen victories. Ken Forsch, Steve Renko, and Bruce Kison combined for thirty-four more.

The Angels wound up winning a club-record ninety-three games and also claimed the division championship. In the American League Championship Series, it appeared the Angels might give manager Gene Mauch his first pennant. (Mauch had managed in the majors for more than two decades with several teams.) California won the first two games of the best-of-five series against the Milwaukee Brewers, but both those games were played at Anaheim Stadium. The Angels still needed one more triumph—and they didn't get it. The Brewers rallied for three straight victories in Milwaukee to win the series and advance to the World Series. The Angels returned

*The sweet-swinging Rod Carew.*

*Rod Carew (sliding)
set an Angel club
record by hitting for
a .339 average
during the season.*

to California as the first team to have blown a two-games-to-none lead in a league championship series.

California was unable to repeat as division champ in 1983, but Rod Carew put on a hitting display that will be remembered for a long time. The Angels star hit more than .400 for much of the season before tailing off in August and September. "The difference between this guy and the rest of us is that when we get hot, we go up to .300," Doug DeCinces explained. "When he gets hot, he goes up to .500." California center fielder Gary Pettis may have summed up Carew's ability best when he said, "Most guys hit when they can; he hits when he wants."

Carew continued to hit for a high average in 1984 and 1985. By the middle of the 1985 season, he stood on the threshold of a batting milestone—three thousand career

*Hard-hitting Bobby Grich.*

*Speedster Devon White*

*Angel slugger Reggie Jackson (right) takes a big, but unsuccessful swing at a fastball in a game against Detroit.*

hits. Carew got that three thousandth hit on August 6, 1975, at Anaheim Stadium. After the game Gene Mauch praised Carew's work ethic as the main reason for his reaching his goals. "Rod was born with great hand-eye coordination, but he worked his rear end off to become a great hitter," Mauch said. "He has three thousand hits, and he's gotten one hundred in practice for every one of those because he's practiced more than anyone you ever saw."

Carew's three thousandth hit was the last highlight of his Angel career. At the start of the 1986 season, Carew was sitting at home hoping the Angels would sign him for another season. But the Angels didn't need Carew, because they had a new, young first baseman whom Carew had helped to develop. His name was Wally Joyner.

**J**oyner joined the Angels during the 1985 season, and one of his first teachers was Rod Carew, the man he would eventually replace. "I used to tell him, 'Here I am, helping you, and you're going to take my job!'" Carew joked. "Wally would give me one of his laughs and have this sheepish grin on his face. I told him, 'I'm only kidding, Wally. I can help you.' That's what we're all in this game for."

*New manager Gene Mauch guided the Angels to a 90–72 record, the second best in club history.*

When the 1986 season began, Joyner was the Angels' starting first baseman, and even though Carew was no longer around to serve as teacher, Joyner had found a new instructor—Reggie Jackson. "I've worked with young players before, but this guy has taken advantage of my teaching more than anyone else," Jackson reflected. "He asks about everything. He wants to learn."

"He's told me about some of his stumbles," Joyner explained, "and how to avoid them. We've talked about handling the good and the bad, the slump that is bound to come and sure to be magnified." Joyner, however, didn't have to worry about any slumps during the 1986 season. In fact, although he was not expected to have home-run power, Joyner immediately became one of the top long-ball hitters in the American League. "No one could have foreseen that this kid was going to hit fifteen home runs in his first thirty-seven games in the big leagues," Jackson said. "But I could see he had the tools." Joyner, however, didn't think he had the ability to use those tools. "I didn't expect to hit fifteen [home runs] the whole year," he claimed. "I never think about hitting a

*Don Sutton.*

home run. Sometimes I sit down, and it doesn't feel like I've ever hit one. I'm in dreamland."

After watching Joyner hit, Angel fans began to think they were in dreamland—or Wally World, a phrase coined by one sportswriter. "He's such a good, All-American kid," explained Angels broadcaster Ron Fairly. "You want to stand next to him in a rainstorm because you know lightning won't hit him."

Led by the young Joyner and a cast of veterans, the Angels rose to the top of the American League West Division and stayed there. While California was winning, many of the players were establishing milestones. On May 14, 1986, Reggie Jackson hit his 537th home run to move past Mickey Mantle into sixth place on the all-time homer list. On June 18, pitcher Don Sutton became the nineteenth three hundred-game winner in major-league history. Sutton also went on to reach two other goals: he made seven hundred starts and pitched five thousand innings. On October 2, Bob Boone caught his 1,807th career game to move into second place behind the all-time leader, Al Lopez.

By the end of the season, the Angels had reached a milestone as a team, winning the franchise's third-ever division championship. It also seemed as if the club would go on to make its first appearance in the World Series, as the Angels took a three-games-to-one lead against the Boston Red Sox in the best-of-seven American League Championship Series. In the fifth game of the series, nearly sixty five thousand California fans showed up at Anaheim Stadium to root the Angels to victory.

And victory seemed almost certain as California took a 5–2 lead into the top of the ninth inning. But then

1 9 8 6

*Veteran Don Sutton became the 19th 300-game winner in major league history on June 18.*

*Left to right: Johnny Ray, Jack Howell, Bert Blyleven, Kirk McCaskill.*

Boston player Don Baylor, a former Angel, slammed a two-run homer to cut the lead to 5–4. California manager Gene Mauch brought in ace relief pitcher Donnie Moore to halt the Red Sox rally. With two outs and Dave Henderson at the plate, Moore quickly threw two strikes past the Boston batter. But with the Angels one strike away from the World Series, Henderson broke their hearts with a two-run homer to give Boston a 6–5 victory. The series, now three games to two in favor of the Angels, then shifted back to Boston, where the Red Sox won two straight to claim the American League pennant.

*Despite the loss of aging slugger Reggie Jackson the Angels recorded another successful season.*

The series loss was particularly hard on Mauch, who had managed twenty-five years in the majors without going to the World Series. Mauch would manage the Angels again in 1987, promising to build a young team to replace California's aging stars. Unfortunately, the rebuilding process was too long for Mauch to take; he quit after the 1987 season. The job of developing young players, such as outfielder Devon White, second baseman Mark McLemore, and shortstop Dick Schofield, would fall on new manager Cookie Rojas. Rojas, however, lasted only one season before being replaced by Doug Rader.

### ABBOTT OVERCOMES, AND IGNORES, OBSTACLES

When the 1989 season began, Rader knew the team's success would be tied to how well his young pitching staff performed. The staff had plenty of talent—Kirk McCaskill, Chuck Finley, and a surprising left-hander named Jim Abbott. Abbott's story is a

*Shortstop Dick Schofield (pages 26–27).*

*First baseman Wally Joyner led the Angels in base hits (167) for the second time in his career.*

remarkable one. Born without a right hand, he still managed to become a top college pitcher, and wound up starring on the United States baseball team in the 1987 Pan American Games and the gold-medal-winning squad in the 1988 Summer Olympics. The Angels shocked the experts by letting the twenty-one-year-old Abbott start the 1986 season in the major leagues. "My Pan Am Games teammates told me not to be nervous about the pros," Abbott said. "They said if you're a decent pitcher, the majors will force you to become a better pitcher."

There was no doubt Abbott could throw the ball, but could he field it? The answer turned out to be: yes. Abbott has developed a technique of transferring his glove to his throwing hand after releasing the pitch. If the ball is hit to him, he fields it and, in one motion, pulls the mitt off his throwing hand with his other, handless arm and then throws the ball to the appropriate base. Abbott does this so smoothly that his fielding is actually considered a strength. "Anyone who approaches Jim as an oddity, believe me, is on the wrong path," Doug Rader said. "Jim is the most *un*handicapped person I know."

Abbott stayed in the Angels' starting rotation through-out the 1989 season, despite his lack of two hands, his inexperience, and the doubts of experts. "If he can look past his disability the way he has," said Milwaukee star Paul Molitor, "then my advice to batters who face him is that they better do the same thing." Abbott wound up the 1989 season with a respectable 12–12 record and a 3.92 ERA, both excellent marks for a rookie.

The Angels also had a solid season in 1989, finishing 91–71, which put them in third place in the powerful

*Brian Downing (left) completed his thirteenth and final season in a California uniform.*

American League West. Starting pitchers Kirk McCaskill, Chuck Finley, and veteran Bert Blyleven combined to win forty-eight games and lose only twenty-four. Relief pitcher Brian Harvey had twenty-five saves. As for hitting, Wally Joyner had another solid year, and so did outfielder Chili Davis, who led the team in homers (twenty-two) and RBI (ninety).

The 1989 season was a big turnaround for the Angels, who had posted a losing record in 1988. Owner Gene Autry was so encouraged by the improvement that he spent $16 million to bring standout left-handed pitcher Mark Langston, a free agent, to the Angels for the 1990 season. Langston, considered one of the most gifted pitchers in the majors, joined a pitching staff already loaded with talent.

*Pitcher Jim Abbott.*

*First baseman Wally Joyner.*

*Led by pitcher Chuck Finley, and a new supporting cast, California completed a dramatic turn-around.*

The Angels, however, did not have a banner year in 1990. Langston won his first start as an Angel, combining with reliever Mike Witt to throw a no-hitter against the Seattle Mariners. But Langston didn't win another game in Anaheim until August. The Angels, who had hoped to contend for the division title, fell out of the race early and never recovered.

Despite that disappointment, the future looks bright. Probably no other team in the majors can claim three left-handed starters as good as Langston, Chuck Finley, and Jim Abbott. The aggressive rebuilding program begun by Gene Mauch has started to pay dividends. Only a few years ago, the team was one of the oldest in the majors; now it's one of the youngest. In addition to Wally Joyner, Devon White, Mark McLemore, and all the pitchers, the Angels have two more potential stars of the future: outfielder Dante Bichette and catcher John Orton.

These players are the main reasons the California management believes the team is on the verge of winning its first pennant. After thirty years loaded with near misses, the Angels are aiming to soar to the top of the American League.